ENJOY GARDENING WITH THE WHITENS

Geoff and Faith Whiten

Published 1979 by Floraprint Limited, Nottingham. Printed in England.
ISBN 0 903001 38 1 (paperback)

Geoff and Faith Whiten are a husband and wife garden design and writing team.

Geoff trained in horticulture as an apprentice for five years with Slough Borough Council Parks Department. He went on to specialise in landscape design and construction, firstly in local authority and later in private companies, in particular the well known firm of John Waterer Sons and Crisp Ltd. For some five years he has been a freelance landscape designer, particularly concerned with the creation of practical family gardens.

Faith grew up in a family garden centre and landscape business, with an additional interest in languages and writing. She has always been involved in Geoff's work, but much of her time in earlier years was spent in bringing up their two young sons, Dominic and Josh, now aged ten and six.

The couple now work closely together and have pursued a joint career in broadcasting and writing. They published their first book in 1976, followed by a Garden Play Pack for children. They contribute regular articles and features to publications for professional and amateur gardeners.

Geoff and Faith Whiten have been involved in planning and exhibiting gardens at the Chelsea Flower Show for several years, and the garden they designed and exhibited for "Practical Householder" magazine in 1978 was awarded the Royal Horticultural Society's Gold Medal.

Their philosophy is that gardens should be thoughtfully and practically planned so that they become a valuable place for family use and enjoyment rather than a drudge.

Introduction

Everyone likes to look at an attractive garden, but sadly few people realise the tremendous potential that is on their own doorstep.

We believe that most gardens could give a great deal more enjoyment, in so many ways. A garden can be a place of leisure — for playing, sitting or eating. Trees and shrubs can be grown to improve your surroundings in the long term, and bright seasonal colour added by gardening with bulbs and annual flowers.

You can go down to earth producing fresh fruit and vegetables, or reach creative heights making spectacular decorative features. Enjoy the ruggedness of rock, the calm of a still pool or the excitement of moving water in a fountain or waterfall. Have fun experimenting with the finishing touches — pots, ornaments and statues. There is a wealth of activity among the wildlife with whom you share your garden, and what better way for children to appreciate the wonders of nature?

We have tried to pack this book full of basic, commonsense information to introduce you to all these aspects of gardening. But there is more, because we firmly believe that a garden should be well planned in order to afford the maximum enjoyment.

The design should be practical, making the garden convenient and easy to run. It should also be beautiful, making the best use of all the available space, enhancing the appearance of your house and considerably improving the view from your window.

For if the garden looks attractive, you will want to use it, and to care for it. We hope that with our help many dull and neglected gardens will be brought to life as never before!

Contents

The planning process

▲
A garden planned to provide attractive living space and an interesting view all year round.

◄
A pleasant haven of cool green. The smooth curve of the stream leads the eye towards the house, and the tree forms a bold focal point. The mass of mature climbing plants blends the house with the garden, making it difficult to see where one ends and the other begins.

►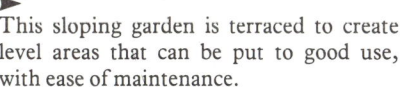
This sloping garden is terraced to create level areas that can be put to good use, with ease of maintenance.

Many people feel daunted by the prospect of creating and maintaining a garden, fearing that their ignorance of gardening methods and the care of plants will mean inevitable failure. Perhaps a little more optimism and positive thinking would lead to the transformation of those lines of boring and neglected gardens that can be seen from the route of any suburban train journey.

We believe that with such positive thinking, and a little practical guidance, it is possible to create a useful and attractive garden — one that is within your reach in terms of time, money and physical ability.

Sophisticated machinery and gadgets have become part of our everyday lives, but our ancestors' survival depended on their ability to work the land, so perhaps gardening as an activity is not so far from being one of our natural instincts! Certainly the creation of gardens as a means of adding beauty to our environment has a long history.

Even before the time of the Roman Empire various civilizations had developed the building of small gardens attached to the individual house, as an integral part of their domestic surroundings.

However, during the Dark Ages following the fall of the Roman Empire there was little activity or advance in the art of gardening.

Much later the Elizabethans created gardens based on intricate patterns; the knot garden is a typical example. These, however, were not small gardens attached to the homes of ordinary folk, but were the grounds of palaces, manors and grand houses.

During the Renaissance period formal layouts on the grand scale flourished in France and Italy and the style spread to Britain. A classical influence was much favoured, and reproductions of Greek and Roman statues were as essential as the elaborate fountains and planted beds laid out in regular, geometric patterns.

The eighteenth century, however, produced a spirit of rebellion against such stiff and regimented formality. Launcelot 'Capability' Brown advocated the creation of 'natural' pastoral settings. These were, in fact, an idealized version of nature — the landscape as we might like it to be — but they have survived and matured to become an essential part of our landscape heritage.

The early Victorian era saw the introduction of the herbaceous border and a growing interest in plants for their own sake. Botanists embarked on plant hunting expeditions all over the world — one such journey gave Australia's Botany Bay its name because of the wealth of new plants to be found there. The fascinating new species were soon named and cultivated, and began to find a place in many garden schemes, again primarily the large gardens of wealthy landowners.

But during the reign of Queen Victoria the social scene slowly began to change, as on the perimeter of the big cities people settled in suburbs and acquired a house with its own garden, albeit a modest plot for many. The change marked the start of a move towards the conditions of today, when most gardens are owned by the ordinary family. Not only is gardening a hobby that is open to most men and women; what is more we have greater leisure time to enjoy such pursuits.

Few of us any longer have vast areas available for the creation of extensive formal gardens, and probably few of us would want such a garden. Not only did its upkeep demand a large, permanent workforce, its potential as a place for pleasant and comfortable relaxation was strictly limited, its main purpose being that of a showpiece. Modern gardens may be much smaller, but they nevertheless present a valuable opportunity for the addition of an extra dimension to our everyday lives.

The Americans originally looked to English traditions for inspiration in the creation of their gardens, but more recently we have begun to accept their approach to the garden as an important part of a family's environment — a place to be used and enjoyed as often as possible.

If the garden is to provide useful

Modern gardens may be smaller now but they present an opportunity to extend the 'living' area outwards from the house.

living space for its owners and afford an interesting and attractive view all the year round, then careful and thoughtful planning is essential. Planning of an interior décor is generally considered important; most people take great care to match the colours of paintwork or wallcoverings with carpet and furnishings. Thought is given to whether surfaces should be plain or patterned, and then to the intensity of the pattern, its colour and the style and atmosphere it evokes. Furniture and fittings are chosen to suit the size of the room, allowing for the comfort and free movement of the people who will use it.

This careful process of consideration and selection is equally important outdoors as indoors. Planning and forethought can avoid so many ghastly mistakes and much resultant despair and disappointment. If an area of concrete is laid and then found to be an eyesore, breaking it out and removing the debris can be a tiresome and expensive operation. It is too late to discover that a tree has been planted too near to the house when its roots have already started to disturb the foundations! Just as interior planning is based around the needs of the people living in the house, so the garden should be planned with your requirements in mind. The space is there for you to use and enjoy.

The planning process
The basic planning process involves reaching decisions on the uses to which your garden will be put, finding the best place for all the necessary features within the limitations of the site, and finally bringing together all these features in a pleasing design. This is true whether the garden is an overgrown wilderness or a barren waste covered in a thin sprinkling of something the builder was pleased to call topsoil. Either prospect can be equally depressing.

What do you want in your garden?
Specialists who wish to devote

their plot entirely to a particular interest will have no dilemma as to the features they wish to include in a garden layout, but for most the choice will be rather less than straightforward.

A clean, hard surface — probably in the form of a paved patio — is a fairly basic necessity, since it is no fun having mud continually trampled into the house. A path will probably be necessary for access from the patio to other parts of the garden.

Most people like to see a lawn; many will want to grow vegetables. A plot should be allocated away from the shade of large trees.

Decorative features such as a pond or rock garden may be considered a high priority, and a statue or other ornamentation can add the finishing touches. Space for children to play may, on the other hand, be considered more important.

Certainly plants are vital. Only the most unfeeling person could fail to appreciate the infinite variety of flowers in colour and form, the texture and movement of leaves and the changes brought about by the seasons. The choice of plants will, however, depend on personal preference and on the conditions of the site, particularly climate and soil.

How will the garden be used?
Ultimately the selection of features depends on how you will use the garden and that, of course, depends on who you are.

For example, a couple or individual with no children at home may have little time for gardening jobs that demand urgent attention, preferring to potter outdoors when they feel so inclined and to spend time relaxing after a hard day's work. Certainly such people will want a pleasing view from the window when they sink into their easy chair. The emphasis will, therefore, be on a good looking garden that does not require too much maintenance, but allows space for sitting, eating and entertaining outdoors.

A patio will be needed and this should be spacious to

Before attempting to plan a garden you must decide how you wish to use the space.

Just a small corner of a garden, but a picture with a lot to say. Mature shrubs show the importance of a planned framework of permanent plants, to give the garden shape and to soften the outline of the house; they give a lush appearance without the use of a lot of colour. The lawn is open and uncluttered, and the change in its level is marked by the clean, simple line of the step.

The architectural quality of *Rhus typhina* complements this modern building, making the entrance more attractive and inviting.

Luxurious leisure: the pool is conveniently close to the house in a sunny position, and has a practical paved surround. The table setting is more intimate, in the shelter of a rose-clad wall.

accommodate visiting friends and family. It would be worthwhile planning for a built-in barbecue and seating to form the focal point of activity on convivial summer evenings.

A lawn may present too much maintenance work and an alternative would be an open area surfaced in pea shingle or a similar material, broken up by ground cover planting. Decorative features would be important; an ornamental pool with fountain, for instance, should be planned close to the house so that it can easily be seen and enjoyed.

As regards planted areas, these would probably consist in the main of shrubs which need some attention, but do not make as many demands as seasonal plants. Busy people may not want to grow vegetables seriously, but they might like a few herbs for cooking, perhaps grown in pots on the patio or in a bed near to the barbecue, where their aroma can be appreciated. One or two small fruit trees would also make a useful addition to the scheme.

Where a layout is essentially decorative, outdoor lighting will extend the hours of pleasure it can give. Individual lights should be positioned to illuminate beautiful plants and objects, or the patio area for practicality.

A young couple planning the garden of their first house should do so with a degree of flexibility if children are intended, for they will soon become a family with youngsters whose needs must be met.

For the family garden a patio is again important, but not only for relaxing and eating. It will also provide space for play and for riding sit-on toys, particularly in wet weather when the grass is muddy. The addition of a roof to part of the patio may also be considered; this need only be a simple construction of timber and clear plastic sheeting.

Play space for children of all ages is vital. For toddlers this should preferably be within view of the house for safety's sake, so a sand pit could perhaps be placed in a corner of the patio. If a permanent one is installed it can be converted to form a pool when the children are bigger. As the children grow older, and do not need supervision, an area may be set aside for play. If equipment such as a climbing frame, swing or slide is used the surface should not be hard paving or concrete, but pea shingle or similar, for a softer landing.

Almost certainly a lawn will be wanted, and this allows further potential for family games and activities. Even a swimming pool need not be beyond the means of the average pocket, since it is now possible to install for yourself a pre-formed pool with sufficient space for children and adults to splash about. On a practical note, the pool should be in a sunny position away from the nuisance of falling leaves.

With growing mouths to feed, a family would probably want to grow vegetables. The plot can look decorative but is really basically a functional item and is best situated away from the house. The tools required for tending crops will need storage space, probably in a shed. An area can also be set aside for the cultivation of soft fruit. Being obtainable in the shops for only a short season, and at high prices, this is useful for variation of the family diet and some types are suitable for freezing.

The selection of general planting will depend on preferences. A basic framework of shrubs can be planned, but will take some time to mature; spaces can be filled meanwhile with annual flowers grown quite cheaply from seed. Bulbs bring cheerful spring colour when little else is in flower; they can be planted each year or left in the lawn area to naturalize.

Children usually love the satisfaction gained from growing something themselves, and it is often a good idea to set aside an area for their own horticultural efforts.

As children grow up and start to leave home, the needs of garden owners change. They may wish to adapt their existing layout, or move to a new house and start afresh. There will be the opportunity to introduce decorative elements that were previously impractical, or to

Allow for the changing requirements of a growing family when deciding what should go where.

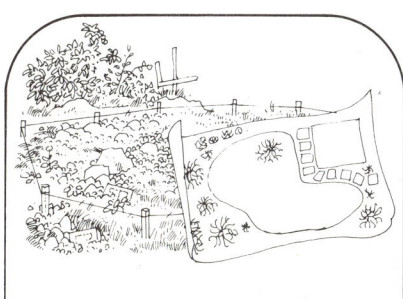

develop a specialist interest — the creation of a rock garden, perhaps, or a large pool for breeding fish.

In later years, when a couple or an individual retires from work, their garden often becomes an important part of their lives, with time on their hands to spend outdoors. However, they must also consider possible physical limitations as time goes on, and the introduction of features such as non-slip paving and raised plant beds may be useful.

Certainly such people would want something interesting and attractive — a raised pool, perhaps. They would probably not be interested in barbecues but may like to take a tray of tea outside on a summer afternoon, and may prefer to sit in partial or full shade rather than bright sunshine. Permanent, comfortable seating will avoid the need to move furniture.

It is doubtful that a large vegetable plot would be required, but space for salad crops would almost certainly be welcomed, and fruit could take the form of cordon bushes, being more manageable than large trees.

As for other plants, one special need that could, indeed, be common to any age group is for flowers and foliage suitable for cutting and arranging indoors. Cut flowers always brighten up the house, and are particularly nice to have around when you are entertaining.

Time and money

The features that you would, ideally, like to include in your garden layout may prove to be beyond your means, due either to the expense or time involved. It is futile and hopelessly optimistic to plan, for instance, for a herbaceous border and a large fruit and vegetable plot if you have only two or three hours a week to devote to the maintenance of the entire garden.

The initial expense and time involved in the creation of a satisfying garden layout is somewhat easier to calculate, and need not prove daunting. Even the most ambitious scheme can be successfully phased over a period of time, tackling the various stages as a series of jobs. It should not even matter if this process extends over a period of two or three years; the vital starting point will have been reached — a plan that can gradually be implemented. Throughout the building process you will have the great advantage of a clear idea of what will finally be achieved.

The site — its advantages and limitations

It is easy to assume that when it comes to the site — the basic material with which you have to work — the new home owner is at an advantage. Whilst life may be easier for him in some ways, this is not necessarily so. An empty plot has no mature shrubs and although there may be one or two trees, these will almost certainly afford no privacy from neighbours.

An established feature in the garden of an older house can provide a useful focal point around which to build. Triumph can arise from diversity, for the very limitations that seemed to make redesign impossible can provide an essential starting point. Indeed, the restrictions imposed by planning around an existing framework can prove easier to handle than the almost bewildering range of possibilities offered by the virgin site.

Consider the advantages that the site has to offer, whatever its condition, and think very carefully before tearing out large shrubs and trees. What is easily destroyed in an afternoon can take years to replace.

If the site offers pleasant views, incorporate these in the design. The creators of the 'ha-ha' knew what they were doing. Only a ditch — invisible from afar — divided the garden from the open countryside beyond, creating the impression that the owner's property extended to rolling acres as far as the eye could see.

Each site has its own particular problems — some have more than others — and the solutions depend to a great extent on the main

1 **Hypericum 'Hidcote'**
2 **Hedera helix 'Gold Heart'**
3 **Hebe anomala**
4 **Escallonia 'Donard Radiance'**
5 **Cornus alba 'Sibirica'**
6 **Berberis gagnepainii**
7 **Fuchsia 'Tom Thumb'**
8 **Choisya ternata**
9 **Senecio greyi**
10 **Climbing rose 'Dublin Bay'**
11 **Viburnum davidii**
12 **Ribes odoratum**
13 **Chamaecyparis lawsoniana 'Columnaris'**
14 **Cornus stolonifera 'Flaviramea' x 2**
15 **Chamaecyparis lawsoniana 'Stewartii'**
16 **Fatsia japonica**
17 **Rhododendron 'Scarlet Wonder'**
18 **Daphne mezereum**
19 **Garrya elliptica**
20 **Cornus alba 'Spaethii' x 3**
21 **Weigela 'Bristol Ruby'**
22 **Forsythia 'Lynwood'**
23 **Rhododendron 'Elizabeth' x 3**
24 **Chamaecyparis lawsoniana 'Allumii'**
25 **Hedera helix 'Buttercup'**
26 **Juniperus x media 'Pfitzerana aurea'**
27 **Berberis thunbergii 'Erecta'**
28 **Hypericum androsaemum**
29 **Calluna vulgaris 'Gold Haze' x 5**
30 **Genista hispanica**
31 **Berberis thunbergii 'Atropurpurea Nana' x 3**
32 **Lavandula spica 'Munstead'**

The design of this garden measuring 30 by 40ft is based on a series of circles; this can be the simplest and most effective way of introducing curves to a layout, for it ensures a bold, positive line. The patio has an angled shape, and is planned to be sufficiently spacious for outdoor living, including a table setting. To the left hand side of the patio is an L-shaped section of retaining wall, 2½-3ft high. This not only lends an atmosphere of intimacy to the patio, but can double up as a seat. One aspect of the layout is that its features can be interchangeable. If there are children under five in the family, the pool could initially be a sand pit, converted later to form the pool; the play area could be a vegetable plot, according to the family's needs and preferences.

The informal look of a country garden is right for the style of this house. Natural paving and walling materials are softened by grass and plants.

Again the harsh line of a path is softened — in this garden by a profusion of colourful herbaceous plants. A paradise for the flower arranger!

purpose for which the space is intended.

For family use a steeply sloping garden is perhaps better terraced. Although this involves the construction of retaining walls and steps, it does create the benefit of level areas that can be put to practical use for growing, playing and sitting. Another problem often encountered is a site that is in the shade of very large trees, making it less than ideal for the keen grower of flowers and vegetables. Even a lawn can be difficult and a pond impossible, for it is covered in leaves all the year round. The best solution is to accept the limitations and plan a 'woodland' garden with shrubs tolerant of shade and mown paths through long grass.

Much of garden design is concerned with creating illusions. A long, narrow site looks wider when it is broken up by diagonal lines. A small, dark garden looks bigger and brighter when light coloured paving. is laid. A lawn looks larger when it is not broken up by pockets of fiddly plant beds.

Soil

The type of soil in your garden will, to a certain extent, limit design possibilities. Plants ideally need soil that allows water to drain away rather than form a waterlogged mess, but not so quickly that the plant nutrients in the soil are washed away before they have a chance to do their work. A heavy soil, such as clay, may not allow for sufficient drainage, whereas a light, sandy soil may drain too quickly.

Some shrubs simply will not thrive in a certain type of soil, and it is wise to bear this in mind at the planning stage. Rhododendrons, camellias and heathers all belong to the same plant family, and they all hate chalky soil but thrive in one containing plenty of peat. So if your house is built on chalk, do not set your heart on creating a heather bank or rhododendron walk!

Climate

You will probably be familiar with the general climate in your area, and the local peculiarities that

result. Hard winters, strong winds and deep frosts affect the plants and crops that can be grown. In Cornwall, for instance, seeds can generally be sown earlier than in, say, Yorkshire and tender crops such as peppers and aubergines can successfuly be grown outdoors without protection.

Northern parts of the British Isles experience, too, shorter daylight hours during winter months and this can restrict gardening activity and enjoyment.

Probably the greatest enemy of people's enjoyment of their garden as a place to relax is wind; shelter from wind can make your patio or sitting out area a more comfortable and inviting place. Of course, the most effective windbreak is the house itself, but a screen of trees or shrubs tolerant to wind may also be necessary.

Bear in mind that if you build a wall four feet high the wind will travel over it in waves, like water, and still prove uncomfortable. A height of six feet would be necessary to be effective. What is more, a solid screen is not always necessary; a semi-solid wall or fence or closely planted shrubs can be equally effective.

Blending the house and garden

A garden can never be planned in isolation; it should appear as an integral part of your home, reflecting the style of the house.

Everyone has an ideal, chocolate box impression of what a cottage garden should look like, complete with roses round the door. But this profusion of flowers that seem to emerge from every corner, clinging to walls and covering paths, would not be right for a suburban semi-detached house. A very modern house with simple architectural lines is complemented well by the use of individual plants with an interesting shape, or of concrete and pebbles, with perhaps a simple pool. If a brick wall is required, try to match up the type and colour of bricks used in the house construction.

All the component parts of a garden should be in keeping with

From a visual point of view, house and garden should be in keeping with each other, blending rather than conflicting.

its basic theme, from structural materials to plants and ornamentation. An elaborate classical stone urn and plinth would be incongruous in the garden of a new 'town house', and a yellow plastic bucket seat would not blend with Victorian architecture.

The style of the garden will also, of course, reflect your own taste. Just as indoors most of us acquire over a period of time items that are, perhaps, of relatively low intrinsic value but immense personal importance, so a garden develops and matures with elements that have a particular significance. Plants may have grown from cuttings given by friends, or may serve as mementoes of people or places. What appears to others to be a useless object may be seen by you as the perfect garden ornament.

The pleasure of building up a garden brings an extra dimension that cannot be found in the collection of inanimate objects, for plants are living things. They not only change with the seasons but mature with the years; it is most rewarding to watch a twiggy little shrub transformed into a stately specimen. Planting can almost always be changed and added to, either with seasonal colour — bulbs in spring, annuals in summer — or with a permanent shrub blended carefully into the overall scheme.

Putting the plan on paper

Having considered the various factors that will be involved in forming a plan for the layout of your garden, it is time to think in terms of the more practical aspects of planning.

It is useful to spend some time walking around the garden, visualizing the general areas that would be most suitable for the features you wish to include in your scheme. Look carefully at it from all the rooms that have any view of the site. It is equally important to have a pleasant aspect from the kitchen window as from the lounge, and the garden takes on quite a different look from the first floor of the house.

When you have formed an impression of the feel of the site, you will need to transfer your thoughts on to paper, in order to create that plan so essential to making a successful garden.

If you have a new house, or have had plans drawn up for improvements or an extension, then you may well be able to obtain a copy of an outline plan of the site, showing the house and boundaries. Failing that, it will be necessary to draw up your own plan and this need not involve complicated surveying techniques.

Use squared or graph paper for the plan and work out a simple scale that enables you to show the entire site on your paper (say, ¼in or two squares to 1ft).

Measure first the boundaries of the site and the house and mark them in. Permanent existing features such as trees should then be indicated. These can be plotted by measuring their distance from two fixed points, each on a different boundary. Indicate too features such as manhole covers, house doors and windows and the line of views that are to be either emphasized or disguised.

When you have built up a complete picture of the garden's outline and permanent features, then mark on the plan the general areas you have decided upon as the best place for the component parts of your new layout.

The stage has now been reached where these disconnected parts must be blended to form a harmonious design. But such a design is unlikely to appear as a product of instant inspiration. It is more likely to involve juggling with many ideas before the right one emerges. Play around with lines and patterns in the form of thumbnail sketches or on tracing paper overlaid on the basic site plan.

It is useful to be aware of some basic design principles. Firstly, plan boldly, remembering that people are your yardstick for the amount of space required. Make the patio big enough to take at least four adults sitting at a table and chairs, and several children moving around without running a tricycle over their feet or bouncing

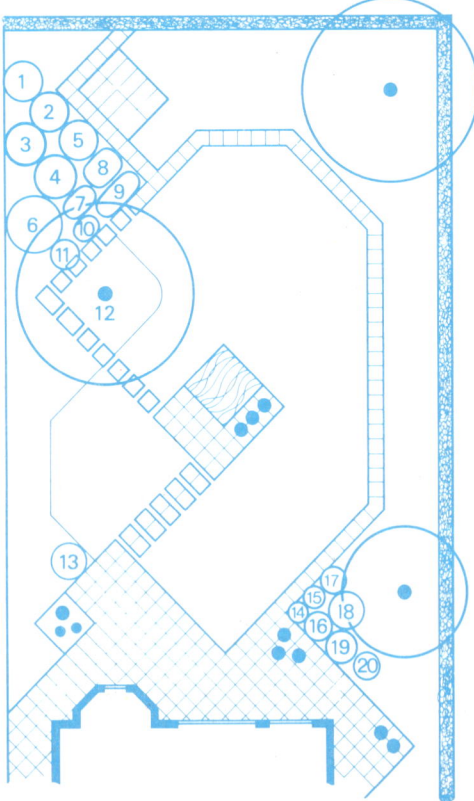

The design of this larger family garden on a site of 60 by 100ft dimensions takes an angled line as its theme. From the right hand side of the patio a solid paved path leads around the lawn edge to give access to the shed or greenhouse or play area. This not only serves as a mowing strip to the lawn, but its solid surface provides a track for children to ride cars, tricycles and so on. The main decorative feature of the garden is a central paved area in the lawn, with pool and planted pots. Its position means that it can be seen and enjoyed from the house, and also serves to draw people into the large garden.

  1 **Cotoneaster simonsii**
  2 **Cornus alba 'Elegantissima'**
  3 **Forsythia 'Spring Glory'**
  4 **Weigela 'Abel Carriere'**
  5 **Potentilla 'Katherine Dykes'**
  6 **Ribes sanguineum 'Pulborough Scarlet'**
  7 **Daphne odora 'Aureomarginata'**
  8 **Rhododendron 'Gomer Waterer'**
  9 **Sarcococca humilis**
 10 **Rhododendron williamsianum**
 11 **Euonymous fortunei radicans**
 12 **Mahonia aquifolium beneath Betula pendula**
 13 **Fatsia japonica**
 14 **Potentilla fruiticosa 'Red Ace'**
 15 **Hebe rakaiensis (subalpina)**
 16 **Hebe 'Carl Teschner'**
 17 **Lavandula spica 'Twickel Purple'**
 18 **Berberis wilsoniae**
 19 **Genista tinctoria 'Royal Gold'**
 20 **Calluna vulgaris 'Alba Plena'**

Imaginative use of a change in levels can transform an odd corner into a delightful feature.

An attractive border; shrubs with delicate foliage are thoughtfully combined with colourful seasonal plants and the outline takes the form of a bold, flowing curve.

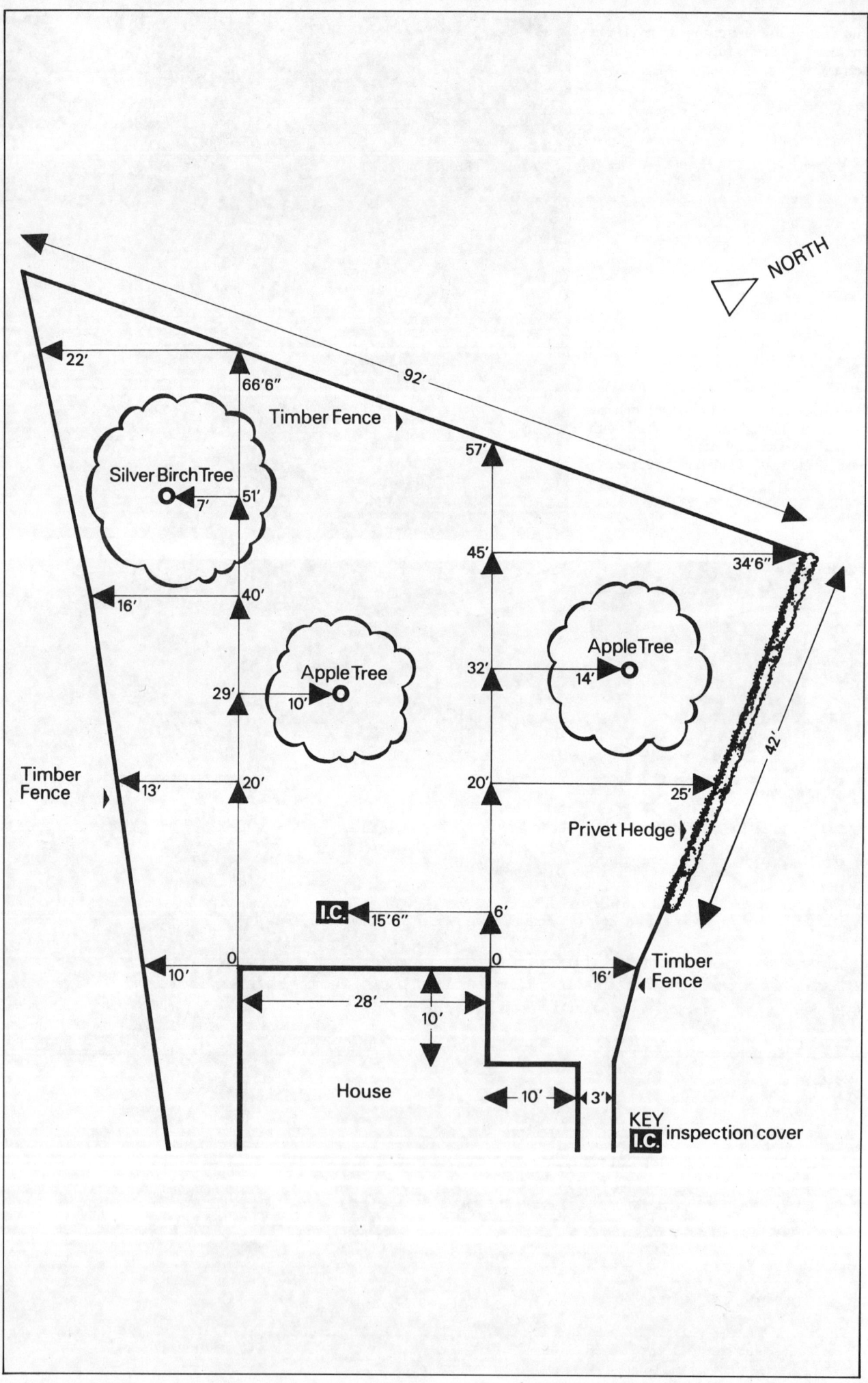

NORTH

22'
66'6"
Timber Fence
57'
Silver Birch Tree
51'
7'
45'
34'6"
16'
40'
Apple Tree
32'
14'
29'
10'
20'
Timber Fence
13'
20'
42'
25'
Privet Hedge
I.C. 15'6"
6'
0
0
10'
16'
Timber Fence
28'
10'
House
10'
3'
KEY
I.C. inspection cover

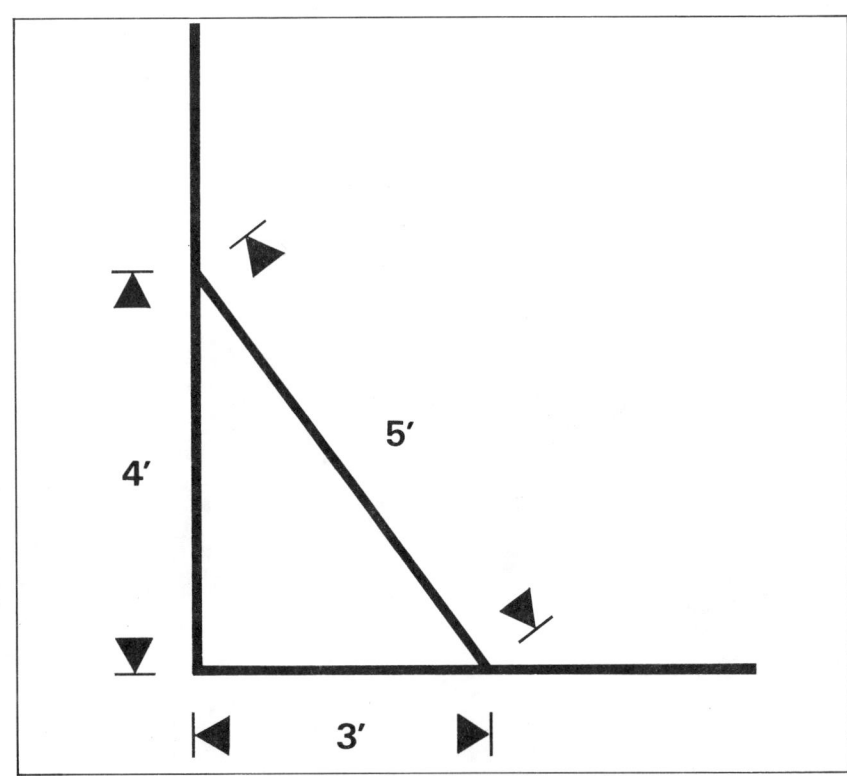

Forming a right angle

It will almost certainly be necessary to mark out a right angle in order both to measure the garden, when preparing your plan, and to put it into action. Use string and pegs to form a triangle of the dimensions shown (or multiples of 3-4-5). A right angle will be formed at the point where the shorter sides meet.

Measuring and plotting an awkwardly shaped site

First measure across the back of the house, and mark the corners of the rear wall in order to plot its exact position.

Measure out the length of the garden at right angles to the corners of the rear wall of the house; if possible run a length of string along this line and mark off intervals of 20ft or so.

By measuring across the width of the garden at right angles to this line it will be possible to plot strategic points of the site boundary, as well as permanent features such as trees.

This is a very basic, simple form of surveying and may not result in an exactly accurate plan. However, it should be adequate for the purpose required, since a discrepancy of up to 6 inches or so is unlikely to cause problems.

a ball into their laps as a matter of inevitability.

Make a path wide enough for people to walk on and seats at the right height and position for comfort. Plan decorative features near to the house where people can see and enjoy their beauty, either from inside the house or whilst sitting on the patio.

Be positive with shapes and outlines; they will appear less stark when transferred into the garden, particularly as plants start to grow and merge with the line of features such as the lawn. If you are planning curves, make them bold. With pencil in hand try loosely flexing your wrist rather than moving your arm in stiff, awkward motions. The result should be a visually satisfying line with a natural, flowing appearance. A curve that is little more than a meandering line or a regularly scalloped edge serves no purpose, and only looks fiddly and irritating when transferred physically to the garden.

Make full use of the space available, attempting to open it up rather than restrict its use by rigid divisions. A straight path running the length of the centre of the plot will not only make it appear smaller, it will also split it into two parts that are more difficult to design. Moreover, if the path leads

to a shed, then the eye will be drawn straight to the shed as a focal point of the layout — not an attractive thought!

This introduces also the element of balance. When both ends of a mantelpiece are decorated with a collection of identical objects, it tends to look uncomfortably regular. It is balanced — but too balanced to create a pleasing appearance.

In the garden the design should achieve an agreeable balance. If each side follows an identical line, a totally formal layout is created, and indeed this can be successful. The average modern garden lends itself better, however, to a degree of informality, but this is where a balance must be maintained so that the end result is not a layout with, for instance, bold curved planted borders on one side and nothing but a lawn running adjacent to the fence on the other.

Plan practically; allow for easy access to the parts of the garden that will get the most use. A large vegetable plot is impractical if you cannot reach its centre without trampling rows of onions. If a shed, seat or greenhouse is planned at the far end of the lawn a path should lead to it, or you will find that a bald track is worn through the grass.

Permanent structures

Brick piers and timber pergola are plant clad, forming a solid but attractive frame for the entrance to this front garden.

Many aspects of a garden can change from year to year. Flowers and vegetables can be grown in a different position and even relatively mature shrubs can be moved. Indeed, many keen gardeners often find the urge to change the pattern of plants from time to time irresistible.

However, structural features such as patio, paths, steps, walls and boundary fencing should be planned to form the permanent framework of the garden. They determine not only a great deal of the outline of the design, but also go a long way towards dictating the style of the whole garden layout.

Your patio garden can be colourful for most of the year by selecting a balance of deciduous and evergreen shrubs, and conifers. The example illustrated here is of a 4.6 metre square (15 feet square) patio facing south-west and viewed from the house. Trained fruits on the fence can take the bareness from the timber — and provide sweet reward in the summer. The wide raised bed adds an extra dimension and allows prostrate shrubs to trail effectively over the wall. Judicious pruning can contain the shrubs once they have matured, to prevent invasion of the patio walkway.

 1 **Cotoneaster congestus x 2**
 2 **Cytisus x kewensis**
 3 **Hedera helix 'Gold Heart'**
 4 **Juniperus x media 'Old Gold'**
 5 **Cotoneaster 'Skogholm'**
 6 **Vinca minor x 3**
 7 **Hebe 'Carl Teschner' x 3**
 8 **Skimmia japonica 'Rubella'**
 9 **Potentilla fruticosa mandshurica**
10 **Chamaecyparis obtusa 'Nana Gracilis'**
11 **Berberis thunbergii 'Atropurpurea Nana'**
12 **Hebe pinguifolia 'Pagei'**
13 **Juniperus conferta**
14 **Juniperus horizontalis 'Glauca'**
15 **Vinca minor 'Variegata'**
16 **Choisya ternata**
17 **Hedera colchica 'Dentata Variegata'**
18 **Viburnum davidii**
19 **Cotoneaster dammeri**
20 **Ruta graveolens**
21 **Genista lydia**
22 **Berberis thunbergii 'Atropurpurea Nana'**
23 **Chamaecyparis pisifera 'Boulevard'**
24 **Hebe pinguifolia 'Pagei' x 3**
25 **Euonymous radicans 'Variegatus'**
26 **Ruta graveolens**
27 **Prunus laurocerasus 'Otto Luyken'**
28 **Hebe pinguifolia 'Pagei' x 4**
29 **Rhododendron 'Praecox'**
30 **Loganberry x 2**

Patio

A paved patio is likely to become the centre of family activity in the garden, and it should, therefore, provide adequate space to fulfil this purpose. If the garden is to be used as an important part of the domestic environment, then it must be possible to do so in comfort, with ease and convenience. To accommodate the normal use of four to six people the patio should be sufficiently large to contain table and chairs, barbecue, planted pots — and still leave room to move.

If a paved terrace is supplied by the builder to the rear of a new house, it is likely to have two major shortcomings. Firstly, an inadequate size and secondly an unimaginative shape, often being no more than a double row of paving slabs running the width of the house.

A patio need not take this uninteresting form. Neither does it have to be a regular paved square or rectangle immediately outside the rear door or close to the side entrance of the house. The paved area can look more interesting when set at an angle, or when the edge is slightly staggered. This helps to integrate it with the overall garden layout, and since a path will generally be required for access to the remainder of the garden, it helps by providing an obvious 'leading off' point for the line of the path.

Certainly integration is an important factor in achieving a satisfying design. It is a mistake to make a small fence or wall along the edge of a flat, rectangular patio. This has the effect not only of making the garden appear smaller by sectioning it off, but creates a barrier in the minds of people entering the garden, so that they feel reluctant to venture beyond the patio and explore the whole area.

In a sloping garden, however, it may be essential to provide a barrier at the patio's edge. It would certainly be required as a safety measure where the ground beyond slopes away steeply.

The position of the patio must be determined as well as its shape. The most immediately obvious place to site it may be outside the entrance from house to garden. This can be convenient in preventing dirt from treading indoors, but is not the only consideration. If the patio is used for sunbathing it should be positioned where it will receive the maximum period of full sunlight, and yet be screened from neighbouring gardens.

Young children in the family will use the patio for play, so consider whether they can readily be seen from the most convenient position indoors. It is impractical to build a paved area that necessitates continually running upstairs or outdoors to check that all is well.

It is equally possible to site the patio at the side of the house, or even in the front garden provided, of course, that it is well screened by a wall, fence or planting.

If all the requirements you will make of a patio are not met by any one position in the garden, then consider creating two paved areas. It is pleasant to have one open area near to the house and a second, more secluded and intimate area, perhaps at the far end of the garden. This arrangement will also serve to draw people in to the garden and encourage them to use it to the maximum.

Whatever its position, there are practical guidelines for building a patio. A strong foundation and level base should be formed, and provision should be made for water to drain from the surface. This is done by allowing for a slight slope away from the house. Where the patio edge is against a house wall its finished edge should be approximately 6in — the equivalent of two courses of brickwork — below the damp proof course.

Damage to paved areas can occasionally be inflicted by a severe frost, causing slabs to lift. These should be re-set to their position once the frost has thawed.

Choosing the patio surface

On moving in to a new house, you may discover the two rather useless rows of paving slabs already mentioned, or perhaps an even worse horror — large areas of

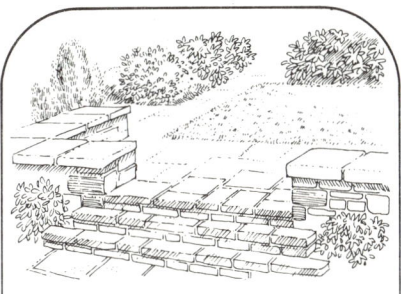

concrete. Even older houses are not free from this problem, for you may inherit an unsightly area of patches of concrete laid at intervals over a period of time. Invariably the patches are cracking apart and providing a home for any number of thriving weeds.

Although serviceable, concrete is rarely attractive. The Americans have perfected a system of brushing the newly laid surface just before it dries, to expose a pebble finish. This avoids that flat, grey, sterile appearance, but it is, unfortunately, rarely seen in this country.

However enthusiastic you may be to replace existing eyesores, it pays to consider carefully the most appropriate material for the garden room that you have planned. The patio surface, will, in effect, be the outdoor floor covering and should therefore be selected in the same wasy as a carpet for the living room. It should obviously be attractive, hardwearing and cost within your budget. In addition its appearance should suit the style and 'mood' of your garden plan and your house. The nature of the material you choose and the size, colour and texture of each module are all important factors in dictating the final, overall effect.

A cottage in a rural setting lends itself to the use of crazy paving in a natural stone, since this is a traditional material, the crazy pattern giving an informal effect in keeping with the surroundings.

A small Victorian house in town often has only a tiny backyard as a garden. If the original brickwork is still exposed, it can be extended into the garden to good effect using secondhand 'old stock' bricks as pavers.

For a newer house modern paving materials can be used, in the form of pre-cast rectangular slabs manufactured from a concrete or reconstituted stone mix. These will continue the clean, simple lines of the architecture.

Of course, your house may not fit any of these examples. In any event it helps to have a general idea of the more common alternatives open to you in choosing a patio surface.

Natural stone

This is the best known traditional material for paving and is often found in rural areas. There are local stones for most parts of the country, although some are more suitable than others for cutting to sell as paving. Natural stone has the advantages of being hard-wearing and presenting a pleasing, rugged appearance, but it is becoming increasingly difficult to obtain and therefore increasingly expensive. This depends on location, however, as does its price, and it is more economical to use a local stone than one that has to be transported some distance.

Probably the most superior and prestigious form of natural paving is York stone laid in a 'random rectangular' pattern, using slabs of rectangular shape in varying sizes. This can be seen on the sweeping terraces of large country houses, but is almost only available today in its most valuable, secondhand state when a pavement is taken up from one of the older streets of a city such as London or York.

Natural stone is more commonly found laid as crazy paving — particularly York stone and Westmorland, Welsh or Cornish slate. The appearance of crazy paving is, however, often spoiled by bad laying. The surface may be uneven, or the stones may be laid too far apart, with large areas of pointing between them. The result is a patchwork of stone and cement mortar. The stones should, rather, be arranged so that the joints are no wider than ½ to ¾in and the overall impression is one of a neatly fitting jigsaw.

Manufactured paving slabs

As natural stone has become in short supply and the price has risen, so the number of variations on the manufactured paving slab has risen.

Some are designed to take on the appearance of weathered stone, with a textured or 'riven' surface, often cast from moulds taken from the natural stone. The result can be quite convincing — a creditable reproduction of the genuine article. Others are very obviously repeats or parts of only one

This small side patio is screened by both trees and a glazed metal framework with brick piers; it thus becomes an intimate area for outdoor living, sheltered from wind.

moulded pattern and a natural effect is impossible.

Although this type of slab has a textured surface, it is rarely non-slip. This is not to say that the slabs are dangerous when laid, but there are slabs with a surface that is specially designed to be non-slip. These are particularly appropriate when the patio will be used by older people or those who are a little unsteady on their feet.

Slabs with a pebble or exposed aggregate finish are attractive, as

they bring variation in colour, and often texture, to the paved area. However, it is worth remembering that they are manufactured from a durable stone aggregate which is impossible to cut in the normal way, that is with a masonry hammer and a bolster chisel. Instead it is necessary to use an electric power tool with carborundum disc attachment for cutting slabs to fit neatly in to awkward corners, around drains and so on.

Manufactured slabs are available in a wide range of square and rectangular sizes, all of them now being sold in metric sizes based on a unit of one millimetre. If a combination of slab sizes is to be used, the pattern should be worked out carefully before the paving is ordered; many manufacturers supply useful guidelines and plan drawings for this purpose.

Hexagonal paving slabs allow the creation of an interestingly shaped patio with staggered edge and

► The planting is certainly bold, but has been chosen to blend with the shade of the concrete slabs and to blur straight edges.

▼ Natural stone laid in random rectangular pattern has a pleasingly rugged and mellow appearance.

provide a more decorative alternative to the square or rectangle.

Whatever the shape of your paving slabs, they represent a long term investment in the improvement of your property as well as your outdoor enjoyment, and should therefore be handled with care.

Always store slabs by stacking them on edge, like books on a shelf. Take care in both storage and handling that the edges and corners are not chipped or damaged, and that the surface of the slabs does not become dirty or stained.

Finally, never throw slabs from a lorry on to the ground. Cracks may not become visible immediately but the damage may be done and will result in disappointment later, when the patio is completed and in use.

Bricks and blocks

The use of secondhand bricks to complement an older house has been mentioned. Where a newer house is concerned, the same principle applies. If brick paving is to be laid, it should ideally match as nearly as possible the brick used in the construction of the house.

However, to lay a large area of paving using traditional clay or marl bricks can be both costly and time consuming, although the end result can be well worth the effort. The very small module results in a high degree of versatility; bricks can be laid in a variety of patterns — herringbone, diagonal, basketweave or even in circles and spirals. The finished effect has a warmer appearance than that of concrete, and can more easily achieve a sense of integration and harmony between house and garden.

Paving blocks share many of the advantages of brick. There is now a good range of interlocking concrete blocks available for laying by the home handyman. These are approximately the size and shape of bricks, but as well as the plain rectangular form are made in the shape of an 'S' or 'V' giving a more decorative effect. Concrete paving blocks are available in a number of subtle shades, but a contrast of more than two colours in one area of paving is overpowering. Such a combination takes on a cluttered appearance that is at odds with the clean line of the blocks.

Concrete blocks are similar in many ways to the traditional granite set, and share its advantages. Although expensive to obtain nowadays, this is an extremely hardwearing material that is eminently suitable for drives and areas that have to withstand heavier usage.

Timber

The disastrous toll of Dutch Elm disease and other tree disorders during the last few years has meant that more felled timber is available; sawn tree rounds make an attractive, rustic material for a patio surface. However, the use of tree rounds as paving is generally best restricted to country gardens where a woodland 'feel' is appropriate.

The timber should be 3-4in thick and the spaces between rounds can be filled in with bark chippings, ground cover planting or even pea shingle.

In a damp, shady position log paving can become covered in a layer of slippery green algae during winter months. Care should, therefore, be taken in the siting of the patio.

Manhole covers

It may be that, having given the matter a great deal of thought, the best location for your paved patio has an unsightly manhole cover as its most prominent feature. However great the temptation, a manhole cover should not in any circumstances be paved over. It is not only unwise but illegal to prevent access to drains. Nevertheless, it is necessary to prevent the cover from spoiling the appearance of the patio.

For the sake of safety and practicality the finished level of the patio should be flush with that of the manhole cover. The obstacle will still be seen, however, and some form of camouflage is desirable. The solution is either to place a planted tub or container over the cover, or to replace it with a recessed cover. This consists of a metal frame into which paving slabs can be set. When dropped into place it is detectable only by a narrow metal rim and small holes for the insertion of hooks for lifting.

Paths

It is a rather obvious, but nevertheless important observation to remember that a path fulfils a basic function — that of enabling you to walk from one part of the garden to another on a clean, durable surface. A path that leads nowhere is less effective, as is one that leads only to the shed when most of the family regularly walk across the lawn to the back gate.

This is not to say that an informal mown path wandering through long grass is unattractive. Indeed, it can be a pleasing feature of a larger garden.

Furthermore a path can be a useful aspect of design, helping to build shape into the garden and to co-ordinate the layout by linking its various features. Planning of the path should be guided by the same principle as that of the total area, so that you work out from the house to the far boundary of the plot.

It is proable that the surface of the path will be required to withstand harder wear than that of the patio, and a different surface may be necessary. Paving stones — either natural or manufactured — are of course suitable for paths, but ensure that the type you intend to buy are sufficiently hardwearing for the purpose, and that they are laid to strong solid foundations.

Where there are small children in the family a paved path is ideal, for it will almost certainly become a track for tricycles, cars and dolls' prams. This means that a smooth, level surface is essential to avoid toddlers tripping on rough and uneven edges.

A path that receives less use — and less wear and tear — could be surfaced more cheaply in an alternative material such as pea shingle or gravel. Pea shingle is quite easy to obtain, either in bulk or in bags, but it should be used

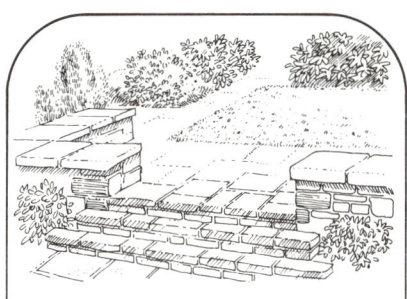

with caution. A shingle surface becomes scuffed up with use and will need to be raked level at regular intervals; moreover the tiny pebbles get inside open shoes as they do on a pebbly beach, and can tread to other parts of the garden.

Because of its tendency to spread, a shingle path should always be edged by a solid border of timber, narrow concrete kerbing or bricks. Although no longer always readily available, the decorative appearance of Victorian barley twist edging makes a perfect finish for paths around an older property. Gravel can be a more satisfactory material, since it consists of larger pebbles in a clay base, which when raked level and rolled forms a solid surface almost similar to concrete. However, some caution should be exercised when the gravel is newly rolled, as it is still liable to be scuffed and carried on to other surfaces.

Stepping stones

As a design feature, stepping stone paths can be extremely useful, particularly when used in a balanced pattern to break up a large, open area of grass. What is more they can be a delight for children, who like to hop and skip from one to another.

However, stepping stones may not be the most practical feature to include in your garden layout. If they are placed in a lawn the grass must be regularly trimmed around them to keep them looking neat and tidy. If you are, nevertheless, prepared to undertake this maintenance work, then you may contemplate using a more unusual slab, such as a circular or hexagonal shape.

Boundary screens

'An Englishman's home is his castle' as the saying goes. Most of us undoubtedly value privacy when it comes to using our garden, and prefer to screen the boundary from the view of the neighbours with a wall or fence. Such a construction will also serve to screen from wind, so that the garden can be used in comfort.

In order to be effective the screen should be five or six feet high, but if you plan to build higher than six feet it may be necessary to consult the local authority planning office. In any event, ensure that your fence or wall will not obscure a pleasant view that you really wish to retain.

On many new housing developments there are restrictions governing the style and height of boundary fences erected to the front of the house, particularly if the scheme is intended to be 'open plan'. These should, of course, be checked and it is wise to keep within their stipulations.

The appearance and upkeep of boundary fences between gardens at the rear of the house can be the cause of bitter disagreements between neighbours. According to the experts, it is vastly preferable to settle these matters as amicably as possible, without resorting to costly legal proceedings. It therefore makes sense to check that you are responsible for the boundary on which you plan to build, and perhaps to notify your neighbours of your intentions. Hopefully this will enable you to iron out any significant differences of opinion before they become major disagreements.

Fences

The garden boundary of a new house is often marked by nothing more than a three feet high chain link fence. Not only is this unattractive, it affords very little privacy.

Where a higher, more solid screen is required, the most readily available form of fencing is timber panels. These are usually sold in a standard width and heights ranging from three to six feet, and the system involves nailing the panels to posts set firmly at regular intervals along the boundary.

The most common design is probably interwoven, with overlapping and other designs also available. They are almost always ready treated with a preservative when purchased. Fencing panels can, therefore, be expected to have a long, useful life, often being in greater danger from stray footballs than the elements.

A more expensive form of fencing, in terms of both time and money, is close boarding. This consists of narrow, individual boards of either oak or a treated softwood; the boards are nailed vertically to a timber framework so that they overlap to form a solid and attractive fence.

A more open form is 'ranch style' fencing. Wide boards run horizontally on palings — often decoratively made — with spaces between the boards. Low ranch style fencing is often seen as a front garden boundary, and has a very modern appearance. Increasingly it is made from pre-formed plastic sections, but if it is of a white painted timber construction it will need regular painting to maintain the clean, tidy finish essential to its good appearance.

Whilst a badly maintained ranch style fence can look unattractive, chestnut fencing is, in our opinion, always unequivocally ugly. This is the fence that consists of narrow vertical stakes linked with heavy wire, and should be used only in its intended context — to prevent sheep from straying.

Walls

A boundary wall creates a greater feeling of solidity and permanence than a fence, and is also more effective as a sound barrier — an important consideration if your house is close to a busy main road.

However, the main factor that deters garden owners from building a long run of walling is that of cost. Nevertheless, once the initial investment has been made the wall should become a permanent feature, providing an attractive backcloth for plants. Indeed, it is important that both walls and fences should be

▲
A simple path of manufactured slabs is made more interesting by the use of brick pavers and colourful planting.

►
Sawn tree rounds make an attractive rustic paving material, but can become slippery in damp, shady areas.

◄
Stepping stones set in grass create maintenance work, but they are a useful design feature. This boldly curved path leads the eye to a patio sheltered by a low wall and planting.

softened by planting; this can take the form of climbers that will partially clothe its surface or of shrubs of ascending height that will blur its angular outline.

Λ wall may offer, too, the possibility of creating an intimate, sheltered area for seating.

The selection of the material in which the wall will be built should be a similar process to that of paving. Again the style and character of both house and garden should be taken into consideration. Where possible a brick wall should be built in the same brick as that used for the construction of the house. If your house is new and the builder is still working close by, you may be able to purchase a quantity of bricks from him, or ask where they can be obtained.

Natural stone walling is perhaps less easily available, but its rugged, weathered appearance has a timeless appeal. It is, of course, best suited to rural surroundings, being a little too rugged and unsophisticated to blend with the urban scene.

As with paving, there are a number of manufactured stone blocks that are cast from natural stone moulds, and are an excellent alternative when real stone is unobtainable. It is wise to select subtle shades and avoid harsh colours, for when used as walling these can be even more difficult to blend sympathetically with the landscape than brightly coloured paving.

Lightweight concrete blocks are a useful material for the modern garden. They are relatively cheap to buy and easy and quick to use. The finished appearance of the naked block is unattractive, and the wall can be painted in a shade that complements the garden scheme.

A further development of the concrete block is the screen block, with an open, decorative pattern. This can be useful where a solid wall would look too heavy or obliterate too much light. Screen blocks are not always used to best advantage in large quantities, and can be more appropriate in smaller sections, used to screen the dustbin, vegetable plot or rubbish area, or even to partially separate one area of garden from another.

There are practical considerations common to all forms of boundary and screen walling. The wall should be built to a substantial concrete foundation, or footing, slightly wider than its base. Where the site slopes the wall should be formed in sections at descending levels, so that it steps down rather than sloping. The footings should also, of course, be stepped accordingly.

For a long run of freestanding wall additional strengthening will be required in the form of a brick or stone pier into which the main part of the wall is tied by means of wire wall ties; these are available from builders' merchants.

A brick or manufactured stone wall often results in an unsatisfactory finish along its top edge, and a coping is required. For a brick wall, bricks laid on edge across the top are most satisfactory. Most manufactured walling comes with matching coping stones and pier caps, and these should overhang the wall by 1 to 1½in on either side.

Retaining walls

If the garden slopes, either away from or towards the house, with a gradient that prevents normal use of the area, then it is desirable to grade the ground to create at least one level space. The sloping soil will then need to be held in position by a solid retaining wall.

For the do-it-yourselfer it is advisable to build a retaining wall to a height of not more than 3ft, depending on the requirements of the site. The wall should be built to a sound footing and should be the thickness of two bricks — approximately 9in. As the wall ascends it should slope slightly backwards into the bank at the rate of one inch per foot; this will avoid possible pressure.

Pressure will build up behind the wall unless you allow for adequate drainage in the form of weep holes at intervals of approximately six feet. These can be formed by raking the mortar right out of a perpendicular joint two courses above ground level. Alternatively a 12in length of plastic hose can be installed to run through the wall.

Stones should be placed around the end behind the wall to prevent it from clogging with soil.

Wall garden

If you plan to build a retaining wall from manufactured or natural 'dry stone' where no mortar or cement is required, plants can be encouraged to grow in the cracks between stones so that they partially cover its surface. Moreover, a low, double sided wall can be filled with soil and planted to form a miniature alpine garden. Good rich soil should be used for this purpose, to support the plants which must, of necessity, be tolerant of dry conditions. Even so, it will be necessary to water the wall garden well in dry summer weather.

Among plants suitable for a wall garden are the following:

Alyssum saxatile
Arabis
Aubrieta
Campanula garganica
Campanula muralis
Cheiranthus (Wallflower)
Dianthus caesius
Dianthus plumarius (and other pinks)
Digitalis (Foxglove)
Geranium
Gypsophila repens
Helianthemum (Rock rose)
Lavender
Leontopodium (Edelweiss)
Nepeta mussinii (mauve catmint)
Santolina (Cotton lavender)
Sedum
Sempervivum (Houseleek)

Hedges

We have mentioned the importance of softening the appearance of a boundary wall or fence with plants. However, you may wish to form a boundary screen using only plants — in other words, a hedge. When mature, a hedge can prove extremely successful as a screen for privacy and peace, and as a windbreak. However it will, of course, take time to reach a mature size.

Consider also the fact that a hedge will take up more space than a fence or wall. It could grow up to about three feet in width and you

Low growing hedges (these do not normally grow to more than 3-4 feet)

Plant name	Comments	Planting distance	Best ultimate height
Berberis thunbergii 'Atropurpurea Nana'	Reddish purple leaves	14in	1½-2ft
Hebe anomala	Evergreen; white flowers	1½ft	2ft
Lavandula spica	'Old English' lavender	1½ft	3ft
Potentilla fruticosa 'Farreri'	Yellow flowers all summer	2ft	3ft
Prunus 'Cistena' (Crimson Dwarf)	Crimson leaves, pink flowers	2ft	4-5ft

Formal foliage hedges

Plant name	Comments	Planting distance
Carpinus (Hornbeam)	Avoid heavy, wet soils	
Crataegus (Quickthorn)	Can be planted alone or mixed with beech, hornbeam, privet etc.	1½ft
		1ft
Fagus (Beech, green or purple)	Avoid heavy, wet soils	1½ft
Ligustrum (Privet) Common Golden Oval leaf	The oval leaf and golden are semi-evergreen	1ft

Informal flowering and foliage hedges

Plant name	Comments	Planting distance
Berberis thunbergii 'Erecta'	Good autumn colour, narrow upright growth	1½ft
Cotoneaster simonsii	Semi-evergreen. Colourful leaves and berries	1½ft
Ilex (Holly)	Makes a good dense hedge	1½ft
Lonicera nitida	Evergreen; black berries	2ft
Prunus laurocerasus 'Rotundifolia' (Laurel)	Evergreen. Light green leaves	2ft

Flowering and berrying hedges

Plant name	Comments	Planting distance
Berberis stenophylla	Evergreen; yellow flowers. Prune after flowering	2ft
Escallonia	Semi-evergreen. Prune lightly in spring	2½ft
Pyracantha rogersiana	Evergreen. White flowers, red berries	20in
Rhododendron ponticum	Common rhododendron. Purplish pink flowers. Large hedge unsuitable for chalky soil	3ft
Roses Hybrid teas, floribundas and old-fashioned species roses	Cut out dead wood in March	Varies according to variety. Check on purchasing plants
Symphoricarpos 'Magic Berry'	Lilac carmine berries	3ft

Conifer hedges

Plant name	Comments	Planting distance
Chamaecyparis lawsoniana 'Allumii'	Bluish-grey	2ft
Cupressocyparis leylandii	Grey-green; fast growing	2½ft
Thuya plicata 'Atrovirens'	Bright green. Trim with secateurs in summer	2ft
Taxus baccata (Yew)	Trim in late summer	1½-2ft

should therefore ensure that plants are spaced well inside your boundary, so that the hedge does not encroach on a neighbouring garden to any great extent.

The existence of a large hedge will also affect the planning of your own garden, for the plants will take moisture and food from the soil, and could cast shade on beds and borders to which it forms a backdrop. This will obviously depend on its position.

If the hedge needs little attention, or can easily be reached from the other side for clipping, then it is a good idea to blend it with planting in the border, by selecting shorter growing plants for the front, graduating to taller plants at the rear. However, if there is no other way of gaining access to the hedge, to trim and maintain it, then allow for access through the planted border.

▶ The weathered appearance of natural stone walling and paving has a timeless appeal.

▶ A retaining wall should slope slightly backwards into the bank. This drystone wall is made more attractive by the use of planting in a bold, dramatic group at its base and in softer drifts at the higher level.

▼ *Campanula carpatica* flourishing in the crevices of a sunny drystone wall.

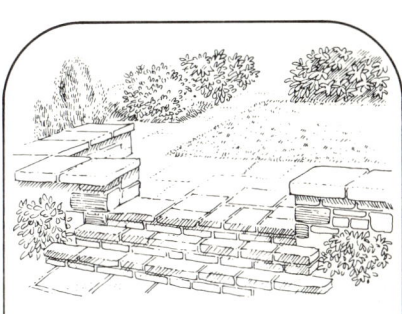

The best known plant for hedges must be privet. Although this stands up well to dust and dirt from roads, it really is used far too often. There are many more plants equally suitable, and their use will bring quite a different 'look' to the garden. Some have attractive flowers and generally make a more informal hedge; they require pruning rather than regular clipping.

A formal hedge with colourful foliage needs to be close trimmed at regular intervals during the growing season.

When hedging shrubs are newly planted they should not be allowed to grow too quickly in height until the lower parts of the plants are bushy and well established. Three or four clippings will therefore be necessary during each of the first two or three years; mature hedges will need clipping only once or twice a year, except where a formal, closely clipped hedge is required.

Renovating an old hedge

If you move into a house with an established garden that has been neglected and allowed to become overgrown, your problem may be in coping with a bulky, unshapely hedge. Think carefully before tearing it out completely, unless you are sure a screen is no longer necessary or you intend to replace it with a fence.

If you would rather renovate and bring under control the existing problem, the best time to do so is in spring — ideally late March. Cut the growth back quite drastically; this may involve sawing thick, woody stems; the sawn ends should be painted with a proprietary wound sealant. Then hose down the lower stems with clean water and clear away all the rubbish that inevitably accumulates at ground level. Finally sprinkle over and fork in to the soil above the roots a layer of compost or general fertiliser; water well if the ground is dry.

This treatment is suitable for a closely knit hedge, where one plant becomes virtually indistinguishable from another. However, it is not really suitable for a conifer hedge, where each plant maintains its individual shape, a screen being formed by virtue of them being closely planted. Certainly it is possible to thin the conifers slightly by lightly pruning the tips of bushy growth, but if you were to amputate the top of each shrub or tree the graceful shape would never grow again in the same way, and their unique, natural beauty of form would almost certainly be destroyed.

Lawns

A lawn can by no means be considered a structural item in the garden, since grass is a living plant. Neither is it strictly permanent in the same way as a patio or wall, since it is always possible to dig up part of the lawn and turn it over to growing flowers or vegetables.

Nevertheless, a lawn can be regarded as an important part of the garden framework; an area of cool, fresh green that can be enjoyed all the year round.

Very few gardens are without a lawn; most people like to see some grass, even if it is only a 'pocket handkerchief'. A lawn provides an open surface for sitting and playing that is softer than the hard floor of a patio. It also introduces a large area clothed in a single colour providing a soothing contrast to the busier, brighter variations in the colour and textures of plants in beds and borders.

The desired effect will only be achieved by a clean, open sweep of grass, and not one that is broken up by little island beds which are, in any event, more difficult to maintain.

The area chosen for your lawn should ideally be quite open and free from the very deep shade of large trees. The soil should drain readily, and not become quickly waterlogged in heavy rain. A lawn need not necessarily be completely flat; indeed a slight slope away from the house to assist drainage is sometimes desirable. It is also possible, and can prove attractive, to incorporate a grass bank where the ground slopes quite steeply or

A well-maintained lawn makes an effective foil to brighter plants but plan boldly and avoid fussy curves and shapes.

to gently curve and undulate the lawn area. However, if you do attempt to achieve an interestingly contoured surface, it is essential to avoid forming dips that will become pockets of waterlogged grass better suited to the formation of a bog garden than a fresh, green, grassy sward.

With the development of modern lawnmowers grass maintenance has become much simpler, but anything that helps to keep maintenance to a minimum is worth considering at the planning stage.

Where a lawn runs right up to a house or patio retaining wall, the construction of a mowing strip is such a consideration. This consists simply of laying a row of paving slabs 9-12in wide approximately 6in below the house damp proof course, so that they separate the wall from the edge of the grass. You will then be able to cut the grass with the mower right up to its edge, and avoid having to finish off with shears against the house. The danger of causing damage to the mower is also considerably lessened.

A new lawn can either be grown from seed or turfed. Seeding means that you can choose exactly the right grass mixture to suit the purpose for which the lawn will be used; a hardwearing one if it is for play or a finer mixture if it is intended to become a velvety showpiece. However, the grass will take some time to become established. Turfing is perhaps more practical if you have children or a dog, and turf can be laid at almost any time of year.

► A colourful low growing hedge of *Berberis thunbergii* 'Atropurpurea Nana'.

► A selection of dainty alpine plants clothes the top of this natural stone wall.

▲
This boundary hedge becomes quite unobtrusive when skilfully blended with mixed border planting. It also serves as a solid green backdrop to the busy colour of the foreground.

There are important exceptions. Never attempt to lay turf when the ground is waterlogged or frozen. Also, avoid laying during periods of drought unless you are able to water heavily and frequently, for the turves may dry out and shrink in size — a process that is difficult to reverse once the damage has been done.

If you have a larger garden and an aversion to mowing, you may consider an area of 'rough mown' grass in which wild summer flowers will flourish. This has its rewards in both the sight and sound of long grass swaying and rustling in a gentle breeze.

Ornamental trees and shrubs

When starting a new garden from scratch, or embarking upon drastic alterations to a dull or neglected site, it is logical to commence with the installation of structural elements. When walls, patio, paths, steps and so on have been built the attendant debris can be cleared and the garden brought into general order. The next stage will be to lay the lawn, if this is included in your scheme, and finally your attention can be turned to the areas to be planted.

The care of plants involves an element of responsibility, almost like the care of a pet, since both are living things with needs that must be met. However, it is a responsibility that reaps rewards in the immense pleasure and satisfaction to be gained from seeing the results of your efforts. This is true whether the results are fruit or vegetables to eat, flowers to decorate the house or plants that make you feel better every time you look out of the window, or smell sweet when you walk outdoors.

Plants, whether they are permanent trees and shrubs or temporary seasonal bulbs and summer flowering annuals, will represent the 'gardening' enjoyment that goes beyond the routine maintenance work of sweeping paths and mowing the lawn.

In order to keep healthy, beautiful plants in your garden it is necessary to create the right environment for them, firstly above ground where choice of site and spacing are important considerations. However, much of the plant is below ground — the root system through which it obtains food and water, and the extent to which it can do so efficiently depends on the condition of the soil.

Preparing the soil for plants

Expressions describing soil as light, heavy, clay or humus are often bewildering to the new or non-gardener, and can leave you feeling quite unable to cope with all the attendant mysteries.

The unfortunate fact is that very few people can claim to have perfect soil in their garden and for most it is a question of improving the soil's most basic problems.

The various kinds of soil found in gardens have been formed from organic matter and decomposed rocks over many thousands of years. The decay of plant and animal life forms a substance known as humus, which gives soil its dark colour. Little humus is found in the subsoil at lower levels because this was formed before plant and animal life were greatly in evidence.

Soil is generally made up of varying quantities of humus, sand, clay and chalk. When these are found in a good balance the soil is known as loam. However, many soils have an imbalance and contain an excess or deficiency of one or more of these elements.

Clay soil is known as heavy, because it is made up of small particles which stick together easily, and do not allow moisture to drain; this results in clay soil being often wet and cold, or in dry weather becoming hard and cracked. Consequently roots cannot easily penetrate the soil to take food, neither do they receive the warmth that many need in order to thrive.

Clay soil can be improved by adding peat, manure or well rotted vegetable compost, which help to form humus, and sharp sand, which helps to make the soil more porous and improve drainage.

Sandy soil is known as light, since it loses moisture quickly. This can mean that the natural nutrients in the soil, which would provide food for the plant through its roots, are

washed away with the moisture. However, a sandy soil is warmer and many crops can, therefore, be planted early in the year.

Sandy soil can also be improved by digging in peat, manure or compost, since this will make it more fertile, and will also help to retain moisture.

A certain amount of lime is essential, as it helps to make heavy soil less sticky and more crumbly and workable. It also creates the right conditions for the release of many plant foods that are already in the soil, and are needed by plants, albeit often in very small quantities.

However, in some areas the soil is so chalky that it is almost white. If this is completely unworkable, you may have to consider importing topsoil, although this would obviously be extremely expensive. Better, perhaps, to dig in a good quantity of peat, manure or well rotted compost.

Warnings are often given about plants such as rhododendrons, ericas (heather) and camellias, which will not grow in a very chalky soil. Whilst this is true, and should be borne in mind, it does not represent a major disaster for the owner of such a garden. Such is the diversity of shrubs that are quite readily available nowadays, that there is almost certain to be a reasonable selection that will thrive in the conditions prevailing in your particular plot.

Digging the soil

Before the soil in your garden can be dug over, ready to receive plants, it must be cleared of debris and unwanted plant growth. In a new garden you will probably have to pick out and remove brickbats and stones, and may even find pieces of wood and tin cans lurking just beneath the soil surface. Weeds, grass and even small saplings should be pulled or dug out, although fine grass can be dug into the soil. As an alternative to pulling and digging, you could use a proprietary herbicide, which will kill only the top growth of weeds, and does not affect the soil. Ensure that this will not be harmful to pets or children; all weedkillers should

be used and stored with caution.

An older, overgrown garden may present a greater problem, and you will need to pull out or cut down larger plants, and dig out the scrub that remains. As a last resort for tough, stubborn scrub, there are stronger, specialised weedkillers available.

It is then essential to embark on some hard work, and dig the soil over. This too is particularly important in a new garden or old, neglected plot, but is nevertheless beneficial regardless of the state of the garden. You will find it easier if you do this in an even and methodical manner, rather than rushing at it enthusiastically and having to give up after half an hour.

Keep your back as straight as possible, use a clean spade that feels comfortable and try to strike up a steady rhythm. Insert the spade straight into the ground the full depth of its blade, turn over the soil and loosely chop the surface to break up large clods.

Turning the soil over to the depth of one spade is known as single digging and is adequate where the soil is reasonably loose and crumbly, and in good condition. However, with problem soils it is preferable to 'double dig' to a greater depth; this really does give plants a better chance of strong, healthy growth. Beneath the first spade's depth you will almost certainly encounter the subsoil, and this should be kept separate from topsoil. Loosen it with a fork, and then replace the topsoil, incorporating the peat or other material according to the requirements we have mentioned.

Planning the permanent plants for your garden

Flowers from bulbs and annuals grown from seed produce colour and interest for just a few months of the year. Certainly they are a bright and valuable addition to any garden, but you would feel cheated if you were able to see only temporary plants, and the plot into which you had invested time and money reverted to bare earth in winter.

The importance of permanent

Always work with your soil and grow plants that are known to flourish in the area and enjoy their success.

30 ft

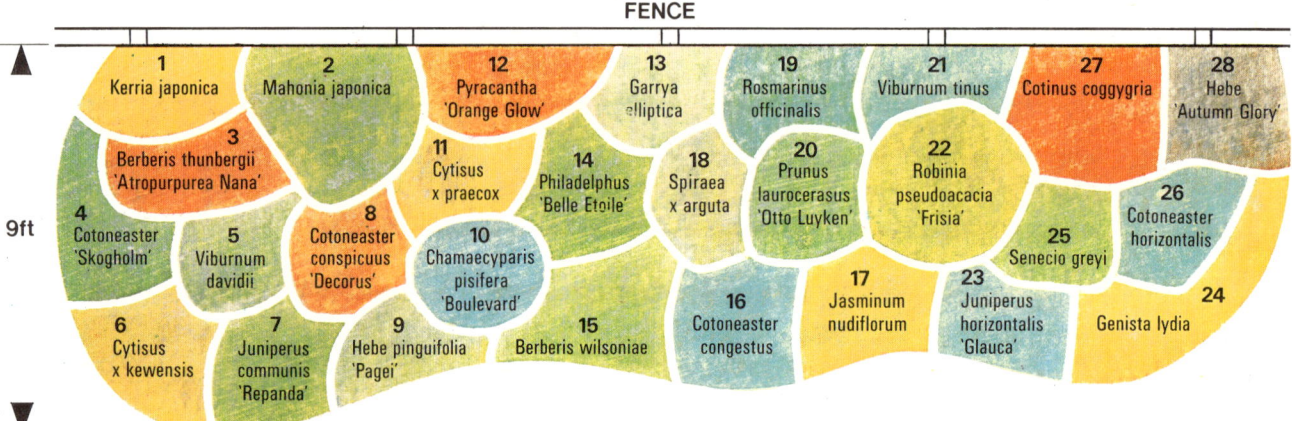

1 Kerria japonica	**2** Mahonia japonica	**12** Pyracantha 'Orange Glow'	**13** Garrya elliptica	**19** Rosmarinus officinalis	**21** Viburnum tinus	**27** Cotinus coggygria	**28** Hebe 'Autumn Glory'

9ft

- **3** Berberis thunbergii 'Atropurpurea Nana'
- **4** Cotoneaster 'Skogholm'
- **5** Viburnum davidii
- **8** Cotoneaster conspicuus 'Decorus'
- **11** Cytisus x praecox
- **10** Chamaecyparis pisifera 'Boulevard'
- **14** Philadelphus 'Belle Etoile'
- **18** Spiraea x arguta
- **20** Prunus laurocerasus 'Otto Luyken'
- **22** Robinia pseudoacacia 'Frisia'
- **25** Senecio greyi
- **26** Cotoneaster horizontalis
- **6** Cytisus x kewensis
- **7** Juniperus communis 'Repanda'
- **9** Hebe pinguifolia 'Pagei'
- **15** Berberis wilsoniae
- **16** Cotoneaster congestus
- **17** Jasminum nudiflorum
- **23** Juniperus horizontalis 'Glauca'
- **24** Genista lydia

A suggested 9 x 3 m (30 x 9 ft) shrub border for year-round effect, featuring flower, foliage and fruit, against a fence background.

General views from each end of the border.

Rhododendrons in flower provide brilliant early summer colour.

plants in the form of trees and shrubs cannot, therefore, be underrated. They form the framework of an ever-changing scene. Once planted, they will mature and become attractive both in their own right and as a backcloth to splashes of seasonal colour.

Since they are intended to be permanent it is essential to plan with care and forethought your choice of plants and their position in the garden. Planning a shrub planting scheme is almost like painting a three-dimensional picture with living material, but plan so that time is on your side.

Most shrubs change with the seasons — some more dramatically than others — and you should group them so that there is always something of interest to be seen.

Colour of plants

Colour is an important consideration when planning. Many people probably think first of the colour of a plant's flowers. Rhododendrons have dark green leaves and a good, bushy shape, but they are not particularly stunning as a green plant. What a different story when the flowers start to appear! Large clusters of tiny blooms in a terrific range of colours from palest pastels to deep purple and crimson. Roses are even less spectacular during winter months, but in summer their colourful, long lasting flowers make them one of this country's most popular plants.

However, flowers are not the only way of introducing colour in shrub planting. Leaves, too, are important. Not only are there more shades of green than you would have thought possible, but plants with grey or silver leaves such as *Senecio greyi*, or the brightest gold of conifers like *Chamaecyparis lawsoniana* 'Winston Churchill'. Some plants such as *Berberis thunbergii atropurpurea*, have reddish or purple leaves; others turn brilliant red or orange shades in autumn, enjoying a blaze of glory before winter sets in.

Shrubs with variegated leaves can bring a lightness of colour and contrasting pattern to a planted area, and even the woody stems have a part to play. Cornus, or dogwood, for instance, is grown often primarily for the dramatic red or yellow twigs that it displays in winter months.

You may wish to plan your shrub planting with a definite colour theme — green, white and yellow for instance, for a cool, fresh look — or you may prefer to indulge in a riot of colour with plenty of changing interest throughout the year. If so, it is still important to maintain a balance, so that there is not an over-concentration of colour in any one area. Lessons can be learned from the basic principles of flower arranging, where strong, bright colours are placed in the foreground and lighter, subtle shades create a softer background. Evergreens are, of course, particularly useful for a constant show of colour that is, incidentally, not necessarily always green. Conifers alone have foliage shades ranging from the silvery-grey of pines to the brilliant yellow of golden varieties of chamaecyparis.

Size of plants

When planning where a shrub should be planted, do not consider the size of the plant you will actually buy, so much as how wide and tall it will have grown in, say, five years' time. This may vary according to the conditions in your garden, but it is still important to allow adequate space for your shrubs to develop properly. A rough guide for planting shrubs of average size is the rate of three shrubs in every five square yards of space. However, the ultimate size of a shrub should be found in a nurseryman's catalogue, or on the plant's label in a garden centre. If you do not resist the temptation to plant too closely at the outset, you may find that shrubs are too cramped to mature properly, and the shape of the plant will be spoiled.

It is perhaps stating the obvious to say that taller plants should be positioned to the rear of a bed or border, and shorter plants to the front. If the entire border were planted with shrubs of a similar size, not only would it appear flat and boring, but the beauty of those at the back would be partially obscured.

However, a 12in high heather would not look its best if backed by a 6ft high forsythia. The jump in size is too drastic to be comfortable to the eye, and height should be achieved more gradually.

It is, therefore, advisable to plan for three approximate — not exact — levels. Position plants 1½ to 3ft high in front, 4-5ft high subjects behind these, and taller plants reaching 6 to 7ft or even 8ft to bring up the rear. The 'banked' effect will look more attractive and give each plant the opportunity to be seen and enjoyed.

If you position just one each of many different varieties of shrubs together in a bed or border, the result can be a piecemeal, unco-ordinated effect. It is better to plan for a mixture of individual shrubs and small groups, to achieve an integrated appearance. Groups should contain three or five shrubs; the odd number makes for an informal but balanced layout.

Position in the garden

Valuable information as to the position and climate in which a plant will thrive should also be gained from a catalogue or plant label. Some shrubs will live happily just about anywhere, but others prefer a certain type of soil or do well only in deep or partial shade or in full sunshine. Some shrubs are tough, and will stand up to windy, exposed sites, others need protection and a little cosseting. It is advisable to choose shrubs that are suitable for the conditions in your garden; not to do so can simply mean cruelty to the plant struggling to survive a hostile environment and disappointment and frustration for you — not to mention the waste of cash!

Shape of plants

It is easy to think of shrubs in terms of fairly nondescript bushes, but the range of shapes in this part of the plant world is enormous. Just consider the difference between the large, flat leaves of fatsia and the dainty, feathery leaves of some of the acers. Moreover a low growing, compact potentilla bears no resemblance to the stately plumes of pampas grass (cortaderia).

Plan your planting to combine a variety of shapes and form, both of plants themselves and their leaves and flowers.

Some shrubs look best in groups, others have a very distinctive shape and are often referred to as architectural plants. Good examples are bamboo, or *Yucca filamentosa*, with stiff, narrow,

spiky leaves and large, white creamy flowers on tall, straight stems. Architectural plants are often used to their best advantage as an individual specimen, taking a prominent position in an open area of the garden. The shape can create an excellent contrast to plants of a less dramatic form if included in a bed or border.

Climbing plants

The growing habit of some shrubs makes them suitable for a particular application. Climbing plants are a good example; they can be used to clothe a wall or fence, to cover a shed or garage that is not particularly attractive, or simply to wind around the front porch. Plants should be positioned in the ground at least twelve inches away from the base of the fence or wall that they are intended to clothe

Lonicera periclymenum is probably the most familiar form of honeysuckle, with deliciously scented flowers, and is ideal for rambling over an object such as a coal bunker or an old tree stump that cannot be removed.

It can be doubly effective to combine more than one climber. Clematis is another favourite, and the 'Jackmanii' variety is a good companion to climbing roses, for when the rose has finished blooming the purple flowers of the clematis take over, prolonging colour and interest over several months.

Some climbing plants need careful positioning. *Wisteria sinensis* has superbly scented hanging lilac blooms, but it must be in a sunny position. The climbing *Hydrangea petiolaris* will, on the other hand, thrive on a north facing wall and is valuable for that purpose.

Jasminum nudiflorum is the winter jasmine, and is useful for colour at a time of year when few plants are at their best. For autumn splendour it is hard to beat *Parthenocissus quinquefolia*, the Virginia creeper. In September and October its matt green leaves turn to shades of vivid scarlet that are quite stunning, and the plant can be grown in a suitable position facing any direction. Finally, ivy is a very useful tough, evergreen climber and varieties are available with green or variegated leaves.

Ground cover plants

The object of ground cover planting is to form a mass of low growing, spreading or prostrate plants so that they mat together to form a dense carpet, thus helping to suppress weed growth. However, before you plant ensure that the ground is free from weeds, and continue to weed the spaces between plants until they are sufficiently mature to mass over.

Ground cover plants are a good idea for a front garden where space is limited and you don't want the bother of a lawn. Plant them in a narrow border where taller shrubs would be too bulky, or in a small area between paving stones to provide soft relief to a hard surface. They can also cover a sloping bank, where bold drifts and clumps are most effective.

Plants that spread to form a dense, low growing mass include *Hypericum calycinum*. Known as the 'Rose of Sharon', this evergreen spreads by mat-like roots and has golden yellow flowers. *Vinca minor* is also evergreen, and varieties have blue, white or purple flowers. *Potentilla fruticosa* has dainty, daisy-like blooms in colours ranging from pale yellow to red.

Other plants suitable for ground cover include those whose stems have a prostrate habit, growing horizontally rather than vertically. *Cotoneaster dammeri* is such a plant; its shiny leaves are evergreen, and in autumn it has scarlet berries. The shoots root where they touch the soil and will spread indefinitely at a rate of approximately 18in per year. *Juniperus horizontalis* 'Glauca' is a prostrate conifer with beautiful feathery foliage on stems like spreading tentacles. A group of three will eventually cover quite a large area.

Selecting the shrubs for your garden

There is an enormous range of shrubs that can be grown in this

Climbing plants and wall shrubs help to blend a house more closely with its garden.

▼
Conifers are invaluable for year-round interest and colour ranging from silver grey to brilliant yellow.

country, and we suggest that one of the best ways of becoming sufficiently familiar with even the more common ones is to peruse a good nurseryman's catalogue. One that gives a description of the plants available and a guide to planting distances, sizes and so on, will prove an invaluable source of reference.

It is, of course, equally useful to take the opportunity of visiting a garden of special horticultural interest, where plant varieties are clearly labelled, for you will leave with a clear picture in your mind of the size, shape and colour of particular plants that appeal to you.

The shape of plants is as important as their colour. The gracefully cascading branches of cytisus are as striking as its golden flowers.

Long Latin names may be found offputting, but they are a foolproof, international form of reference and their use avoids possible confusion when a plant has several different common names, or where there are numerous varieties of one shrub, such as berberis. The name also gives information about the plant itself in many instances, such as 'variegata', meaning a variegated leaf, 'aurea' meaning gold coloured or 'nana' meaning small.

Most shrubs, although not native to our shores, have been with us for many years, and new types or 'cultivars' are rarely introduced. However, roses are being bred as a continuous process, and each year sees a crop of fresh introductions. Part of the enjoyment of rose growing is to keep up with exciting newcomers as well as old favourites. The popularity of 'Peace' and 'Queen Elizabeth' is unlikely ever to wane, and yet a new rose like the miniature 'Royal Salute', marking the Royal Silver Jubilee can have equal appeal.

Planting a container grown shrub or rose

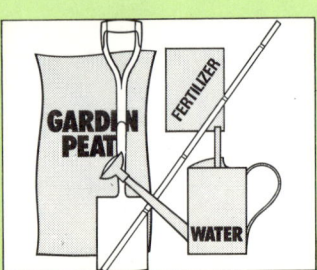

1. You will need
   a. Spade
   b. Watering can
   c. A cane
   d. Peat
   e. General fertilizer

2. Ensure plant is still moist.

3. Mix together equal parts of moist peat and soil plus a little general fertilizer.

4. Dig hole large enough to hold the plant. Mix in prepared compost into base of hole.

5. To check if hole deep enough, place a cane across hole – the soil surface in the container should be about 2.5 cm (1") below the cane.

6. Remove container from plant and place in position.

7. Fill in remaining space with compost mixture and firm.

8. Leave a slight hollow around plant. Water well. If planting in dry weather keep plant regularly watered until it is established.

Where to buy shrubs

If you feel that you have an inadequate knowledge of plants, it is a good idea to go along to your local nursery or garden centre and peruse their stock before reaching final decisions.

You should not allow your ignorance to prevent you from asking the advice of a knowledgeable plant salesman. If the establishment does not include such a person, then you would probably be well advised to take your custom elsewhere.

It is unfortunate that most of us do not expect to be familiar with the workings of machinery that we buy — a washing machine for instance — and yet we feel a sense of guilt and reluctance to admit an unfamiliarity with plants. If more questions were asked at the time of buying, then a great deal of later disappointment would be avoided.

Shrubs can be obtained by mail order from a reputable nursery, preferably one that offers a guarantee of replacement within a limited period, provided that the plant's failure is not due to your negligence. Generally speaking, you get what you pay for when buying plants and if you see them advertised at very low prices, as conifers for hedging often are, then it is wise to be aware that the plants you receive will probably be very small indeed.

Many garden centres offer a guarantee similar to that of nurserymen. Shrubs on display should look fresh and healthy and well cared for, and not give the impression that they have been waiting to be sold for some time without proper attention.

Garden centre shrubs are almost always in containers, or have their roots 'balled' or tied up with a quantity of soil that surrounds them and secured in hessian or a similar material. The soil in a container should not look or feel as though it has been allowed to dry out completely. A 'container grown' plant is preferable to one that has only recently been placed in a container and is known as 'containerised'. The shrub will have been able to establish a good root system and will therefore withstand better the inevitable shock of being transplanted. When you look around a garden centre, if you pick a plant up gently by its stem and the plant comes away from the soil in the container, then it has only recently been potted and should be avoided.

It is beneficial to apply a proprietary general purpose fertiliser seven to ten days before planting. Use a quantity in accordance with the instructions on the pack you purchase. Adding twice the quantity will not necessarily give you plants that are twice as large, and could be positively harmful!

Container grown shrubs can be planted at any time of year, except when the ground is waterlogged or frozen. Keep the soil in the container moist until you are ready to plant and if the soil is very dry in the garden, then water the area where the plant is to go, and continue to water regularly until the plant is well established.

To plant the container grown shrub, water the container and leave to drain, then carefully slit

Planting a bare root shrub or rose and rootballed conifer

1. You will need
   a. Spade
   b. Fork
   c. Peat
   d. Bonemeal
   e. Bucket of water
   f. Secateurs
   g. A cane

2.
Mix together two spade-fuls each of soil and moist peat plus a handful of bonemeal.

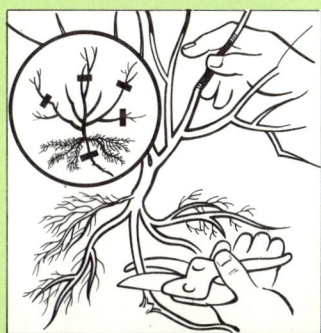

3. With sharp secateurs cut off any damaged roots. Shorten extra long roots to about 20 cm (8 in). Do not remove healthy, fibrous root. Cut back branches by $\frac{1}{3}$.

4. If roots are dry, soak in water for 5-10 minutes. Until planted, protect from wind and sun.

5. Dig hole large enough to accommodate outstretched roots and to the depth of the soil mark on the stem. Fork over bottom of hole. A cane placed across top of hole allows a check on planting level.

6. After positioning, fill in around roots with soil mixture, gently shaking the plant up and down, allowing soil to settle amongst roots.

7. Firm as you fill in. If planting in dry weather keep plant regularly watered until it is established.

8.
When planting a root-balled conifer or ever-green first follow steps 2, 4 and 5. Avoid breaking the rootball.

9. Position plant in hole. If roots extend <u>through</u> the rootwrap netting untie the rootwrap to prevent strangulation, but do <u>not</u> remove wrapping from the rootball.

10. If rootball is wrapped in plastic remove rootwrapping completely, leaving rootball intact.

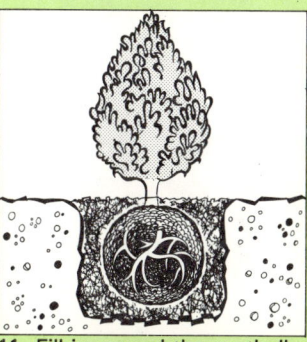

11. Fill in around the rootball with soil mixture. Firm as you fill in. In spring spray foliage with clean water 2-3 times a week in dry weather to reduce moisture loss. Always keep newly-planted trees well watered.

around the circumference of its base, taking care to disturb the roots as little as possible. Place the container in the planting hole, then slit the sides and remove the remains of the container. Fill in around the roots with fine soil, not large clods, and firm. The level of the top of the soil in the container should be just below the finished soil level.

When it comes to planting root balled shrubs, carefully untie the hessian in which the roots and soil are wrapped. If the soil remains intact in a firm ball, as is desirable, then this should simply be planted in the ground, in a similar manner to a container grown plant, and the hessian discarded. However, if the root ball starts to crumble, carefully lift hessian and plant and place in the prepared hole; the hessian will eventually rot away. Nowadays shrubs are sometimes root balled in a plastic material similar to hessian, and this should always be removed before planting.

'Bare root' shrubs are lifted straight from the open ground in which they have been grown, and if ordered through the post are generally delivered wrapped in damp peat and waterproof protection. If the ground is frosty or waterlogged when they arrive, store them unopened in a cool, airy place such as a shed. In prolonged periods of adverse conditions, open the root package and cover them with an open weave material such as sacking, slightly dampened.

The planting season for bare root

shrubs is from October to March. When you are ready to plant, dig a hole of generous proportions in comparison with the expanse of the roots. Normally a depth of 15in to 18in and a diameter of 2 to 3ft should be adequate. Place the roots of the plant in the hole and fill in with fine soil, working it around the roots and gently firming at intervals to avoid air pockets forming. Finally, firm the surface of the soil and water.

Trees

It is easy to take trees for granted. If you live in the suburbs of a large town or in a rural area, you tend to become accustomed to seeing trees around. It is often not until we spend a lot of time in the centre of a large city where there are few trees that we realise just how precious and how beautiful they are. Trees have a special appeal that is quite different from smaller plants; their size gives them an aura of grace and splendour, and the enormous variety of colour and pattern in bark, leaves and flowers creates ever-changing interest.

This is true not only in parks, streets and woodland, but equally in gardens, for a tree has a special part to play in a garden layout.

▶
Climbing plants can clothe and soften a wall or fence. For autumn splendour the Virginia creeper is hard to beat.

◀
Yucca filamentosa has a distinctive, architectural shape and as an individual specimen creates both a focal point and a contrast to plants of less dramatic form.

▶
Ground cover planting; low growing plants mat together to form a dense carpet, helping to reduce maintenance by suppressing the growth of weeds.

Firstly, its appearance when viewed from the house adds height to the vista, creating interest on a level with the upstairs windows; this can be particularly useful if the naked, unbroken view is one that you would rather not see — in town it might be the gas works or a factory and on a new estate simply the open backs of rows of houses.

In the garden itself a tree gives shelter from wind and can help to absorb sound. Its branches cast shade and dappled leafy patterns on the ground, and the soft rustling of its leaves in the gentle wind is soothing and evocative.

Of course, leaves are not the only attraction; bark can be beautiful both in texture and colour; the mottled grey of the familiar silver birch tree is a good example. Flowers are a major attraction, particularly in spring when the ornamental cherries, plums and others are laden with blossom, sometimes sweetly scented.

The vivid hues of autumn bring yet another kind of pleasure, and what child can resist scuffling along through fallen leaves? Even in winter the stark, bare branches of deciduous trees have a dramatic appeal, particularly after a heavy fall of snow.

It is, of course, not only by virtue of their beauty that trees are a vital part of our everyday lives, for by the process of photosynthesis they absorb carbon dioxide from the air and produce life-giving oxygen.

Sadly, the number of trees growing in the British Isles has decreased during the last few years, due to a number of causes. These include the development of land for housing and roads and that now familiar enemy Dutch Elm disease, which has taken such a terrible toll, although it is by no means the only fatal disease from which trees can and do suffer.

It is, therefore, most important that we make every effort to plant new trees wherever space permits. Although, unless you have a large garden, you are unlikely to have space for more than one or two trees, it is also worth bearing in mind the fact that the greater the variety of trees we plant, the better. Dutch Elm disease has shown only too clearly that the elm

How to plant and stake a tree

1. You will need
   a. Spade
   b. Fork
   c. Stake
   d. Two tree ties
   e. A cane
   f. Bucket of water
   g. Peat
   h. Bonemeal

2. Until planted, protect roots from wind and sun. If dry, soak in water for 5 minutes.

3. Remove the turf, leaving a circle of soil about 1.2m (4ft) across.

4. Dig hole large enough to accommodate outstretched roots and to the depth of the soil mark on the trunk. Fork over bottom of hole.

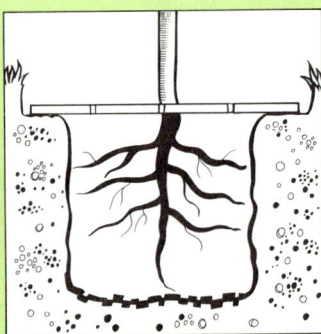

5. A cane placed across the top of the hole allows a check on planting level.

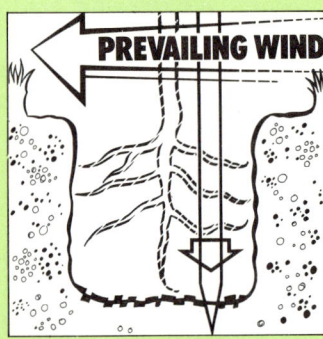

PREVAILING WIND

6. Mix peat in the base of the hole and drive stake in firmly before repositioning tree.

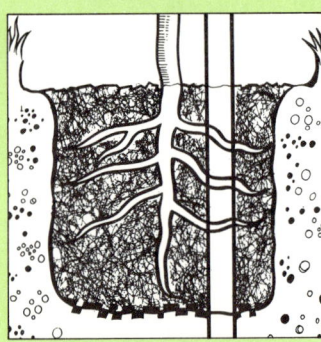

7. After positioning, fill in around the roots with a mixture of moist peat and soil to which a handful of bonemeal is added.
Gently shake tree up and down, allowing soil to settle amongst roots. Firm as you fill in.

8. A final firm with the heel.

9. Two tree ties are necessary, one just below the head of the tree and one about 45cm (1½ft) above soil level.

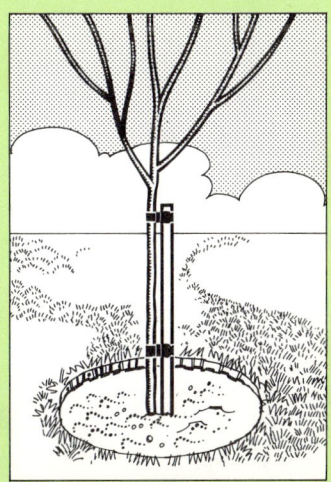

10. Tree correctly planted.

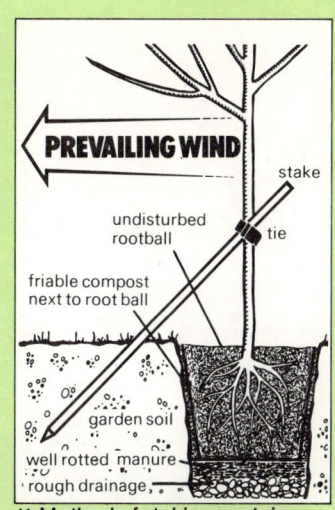

PREVAILING WIND

stake

undisturbed rootball

tie

friable compost next to root ball

garden soil

well rotted manure

rough drainage

11. Method of staking container-grown tree or conifer to avoid breaking the rootball. Can also be used for tall shrubs, to prevent wind rocking.

is just one of the trees that has been planted in concentration in the past. A wide variety of trees will go some way towards securing the future healthy development of the maximum number, for it is essential to see the planting of a tree as a long-term venture.

The importance of long-term planning of tree planting cannot be over-emphasised. You do not have to look far to see the results of ignorance and bad planning that has occurred from five to ten years previously. The branches of a tree planted too close to the house may have dislodged the gutter or roof tiles, and in strong winds there is the danger of damage to windows.

Roots, too, can cause damage. If the tree is close to the house they may disturb its foundations, causing walls to crack. Therefore, when deciding on the position of trees in your garden layout, plan to plant at a safe distance from the house; we recommend a minimum of 16 to 20ft as a general rule, depending on the size of the tree.

A further practical consideration is that of avoiding planting too close to a manhole cover, as in time the tree's roots could disturb the drains themselves. The roots of a willow tree which are, of course, particularly prone to seek out water, have been known to penetrate a drain and start to cause a blockage.

Choose a tree that is appropriate for your garden, both in size and speed of growth. A *Cupressocyparis leylandii* may look harmless enough when you buy it, at two or three feet tall, but it can be expected to grow at a rate of anything up to three feet per year in the right conditions, and you could soon be overwhelmed by its height.

Size is not the only characteristic to consider. Laburnum trees should not be planted where young children play, as the seeds are poisonous. Falling leaves can cover a very small garden, and a large leafed tree will tend to make the job of clearing easier than one with a multitude of tiny leaves that curl up and seem to find their way into every nook and cranny.

A mistake sometimes made is to plant a malus (crab-apple) tree,

too close to a path or, in a front garden, to the pavement. In autumn the fruit falls on the path or pavement and can be messy or even dangerous underfoot.

Planting a tree

Before planting a tree the soil should be dug and prepared in the way we have described for shrub planting, but the addition of some damp peat to the soil during the tree planting process will be beneficial.

Planting a tree is, in fact, a similar process to that of shrub planting, although a larger hole will obviously be needed to accommodate the roots, whether the tree is open ground, root balled or container grown.

When the hole has been dug, bang a good stout stake firmly into the ground, so that a depth of 18 to 24in is below the soil. The tree should then be placed in the hole beside the stake, without damaging the roots.

If the tree is container grown, the container should be removed and the soil replaced around the roots and gently firmed. If it is an open ground tree, with fibrous roots exposed, sprinkle fine soil around them, gently firming as you fill. The finished level of the soil should be in line with the original planting level in the nursery; this can usually be seen clearly from the colour of the bark.

Attach the tree to the stake at two points; one 12-18in above the ground and one at the top of the stake, just below the branches. This should be done by means of proper tree straps or ties, since these can be adjusted as the tree grows and the girth of its trunk expands.

If the tree is planted in a lawn, allow a circle of bare earth around its trunk that has a minimum diameter of 4ft, and keep this area clean and free from weeds.

Finally, a word about watering. A tree needs plenty of water immediately after planting and right through its first summer. Water in the evening, giving a good soaking rather than a gentle sprinkling.

Trees suitable for small gardens

include the following:

Acer negundo 'Variegatum'. Acers are commonly known as maples; negundo is a smallish tree growing to approximately 20ft high, and has bright green leaves with silver variegation.

Acer platanoides 'Drummondii' is slightly smaller than 'Goldsworth Purple' and has striking variegated leaves, which are green with a broad cream border; a very attractive tree.

Acer platanoides 'Goldsworth Purple' is a tough tree that grows quite quickly to reach a height of about 25ft. The leaves are a rich shade of dark purple all summer and the 'keys' are bright red.

Betula pendula 'Youngii'. 'Young's Weeping Birch' grows to approximately 15ft high, with weeping branches that form a dome shape, almost touching the ground. Birch is not fussy about soil, and can, therefore, be useful on poor, light soil.

Malus floribunda. 'Japanese crab-apple' grows to approximately 20ft tall, with a slightly weeping shape. Flowers in the spring are deep red in bud, opening pale pink and turning white, and in autumn the tree produces small, cherry-like fruit.

Malus tschonoskii. This rarely has fruits, but is a beautiful, upright tree with leaves that turn to bright hues of red, bronze, purple and yellow in autumn.

Other varieties of malus particularly suited to small gardens include 'Golden Hornet', an upright tree with white flowers and yellow fruit, and 'Red Jade', a form with pendulous branches.

Prunus trees include ornamental flowering almonds, peaches, plums, sloes and cherries. Trees thrive on a limy, well drained soil. All the flowering plums have purple leaves and pink flowers in varying shades. They grow to approximately 20ft tall, and all are

suitable for a small garden.

Flowering cherries grow to 20-25ft tall, and include the following attractive trees:

Prunus 'Amanogawa', the 'Lombardy poplar cherry'; a tall, straight tree with scented pale pink blossom.

Prunus 'Kanzan'; has a stiff, upright habit and in May bears large clusters of double pink flowers.

Prunus subhirtella 'Autumnalis' flowers in late autumn, with white flowers that become tinged with pink.

Prunus subhirtella 'Pendula Rosea'. This tree has long, sweeping branches, clothed in April with double pink flowers.

Robinia pseudoacacia 'Frisia'. A beautiful tree that grows to approximately 20ft tall, with delicate, bright yellow leaves all through the summer, the leaves becoming tinged with coppery shades in autumn, and the tree producing bright red thorns. This tree needs an open site, with regular sunshine, in order to maintain the light colour of its leaves.

Sorbus aria 'Lutescens'. A variety of whitebeam with leaves that are silvery grey in spring, turning to green in summer. A somewhat larger tree growing to 30ft or more.

Sorbus aucuparia. The mountain ash or rowan tree grows to 20-30ft tall, and has feathery leaves, silvery grey bark and orange berries in autumn.

►

Acer platanoides 'Drummondii' — a compact, attractive tree suitable for the small garden.

◄

Flowers are a major attraction of trees, particularly in spring, when the ornamental cherries and plums are laden with blossom, sometimes sweetly scented.

►

A tree can add height and interest to an open vista.

Short term effects

Annual and biennial plants are valuable in the garden for providing bright, colourful interest in a short space of time. This enables the owner of a newly established garden to fill large spaces between small, young shrubs, or to make use of a bed that has not yet been permanently planted.

An annual is grown from seed and is, by definition, a plant that completes its life cycle within one year. This means that during its growing season — which may be only four or five months — the plant develops from seed, flowers, ripens fresh seed and dies.

In gardening terms, annuals generally embrace also biennial plants, sown in spring and in flower the following spring — and plants which are simply too tender to survive the British winter.

If you plan to sow or plant annuals in your garden, give a little thought to the colour and shape of the flowers, and consider whether they will complement each other and the existing plants. For instance, a shrub with soft, delicate pink flowers would be overwhelmed by a splash of stiff red salvias planted beneath its spread. On a more basic note, plan the height of flowers so that a splendid display of alyssum three or four inches high is not hidden behind towering antirrhinums two feet tall.

The Victorians were very keen on formal, carpet bedding, and we are all familiar with the massed, fruit salad effect of bedding plant layouts in parks and public gardens. Whilst these are attractive in their way, it would perhaps be a mistake to attempt to emulate them in a small, modern garden. Where a large area is to be filled with annuals, choose a colour scheme using just a small number of different plants, and avoid regimenting the plants in straight lines.

The short life of annuals can be turned to good advantage in this context, for it is possible to plant a bed of soft, delicate flowers in shades of pink, lavender, blue and white one summer, and transform it to a vibrant splash of red, orange and yellow the following year.

However, where the plants are intended to fill only a small space, it is better to use one variety rather than a busy mixture. This can be effective both in making a focal point in the overall planting scheme or continuing the colour theme of shrubs and permanent plants. White petunias can, for instance, enhance silver foliage plants whilst purple petunias follow through the darker shades of lavender or blue-grey foliage conifers.

Annuals do not only provide colour in the garden; many are suitable to grow for cut flowers. If you are a keen arranger it is worth setting aside an area for this purpose. Informal flowers with a sturdy stem are particularly useful, and favourites include sweet peas, stocks, larkspur and nigella (love-in-a-mist).

Flower arranging material can be supplied on an 'everlasting' basis if you grow a selection of flowers suitable for drying. These include statice, lunaria (honesty), helichrysum and poppies, which are grown for their seed heads.

The blooms should be picked when the flowers first open. Strip the leaves from the stem, tie them up in small bunches and hang them upside down in a dry, airy place. The flowers should be allowed to dry completely before use, but when they are ready will make attractive arrangements in subtle colours. Useful to have around at Christmas time, when fresh flowers are scarce, 'everlasting' flowers can also be carefully combined with candles and dried or painted leaves to make an unusual table decoration.

The clever use of annuals fills gaps when a garden is new and provides a welcome splash of colour.

How to grow annuals and biennials

Annuals and biennials can be grown quite cheaply from seeds, or you can buy young bedding plants in small pots or trays from garden centres, shops and nurseries. The best buy is plants that look strong and healthy and are not yet showing colour.

These can generally be planted out as soon as they are purchased in early summer, but if the spring has been particularly late, wait until all signs of frost have passed. To remove annuals from their tray, break off each plant with a neat section of soil and place in a prepared hole. Firm the soil around the plant and water well.

Annuals are not difficult to grow from seed, but they require two basically differing treatments. Some are known as hardy and can be sown directly into the soil outdoors, where they are to grow, either in spring or the previous autumn. Others are half-hardy and must be sown in the protection of a house or greenhouse in spring and transplanted into the garden in early summer.

When sowing seeds outdoors, the soil should not be soaking wet. It should, however, be quite fine and free from large stones, and should contain some organic material such as peat or vegetable compost and a little general fertiliser (too much can produce all leaves and no flowers). Tread the soil to firm, then rake the surface so that it is smooth and loose. Scatter small seeds on the soil, covering lightly with topsoil. Larger seeds, such as nasturtiums, should be planted from ½ to 1in deep. Lightly firm the soil.

It is important to thin the seedlings as soon as they are large enough to handle. Pull out weaker and smaller plants to allow the stronger ones sufficient space to develop properly. The distance required between plants obviously depends on their ultimate size. If you are growing flowers from seed, this information will be supplied on the seed packet.

Biennials are sown directly into the soil outdoors in late spring or early summer. It is necessary to set aside a small area as a 'nursery' bed, where the seedlings can be transplanted and grown on until autumn or the following spring. The young plants should then be positioned in the garden, where they are to flower. Flowers will be produced approximately twelve months after the seed was sown.

Seeds that need to be sown indoors require a seed sowing compost, available from garden shops. Seed pots or trays with small drainage holes should be filled with the compost and lightly firmed. Water well using a fine rose on the can. Allow to drain. Sow the seed thinly and cover with a layer of compost that is equal in thickness to the diameter of the seed. Tiny seeds, such as lobelia and begonia, do not require any covering.

Cover with glass or polythene and stand in a warm place until the seedlings germinate and show through. They should then be uncovered and transferred to a light position. When the seedlings are large enough to handle, transplant them into individual pots — peat pots are ideal — or trays, with 1½in between plants. These should be filled with potting compost.

They can be planted out in the garden when all danger of frost has passed, but should first be hardened off gradually to ensure that they are fully acclimatised. This can be done by putting the plants outdoors in the daytime and taking them in at night, until the nights are a little warmer and the plants can be left out all night.

All annuals should be grown in a position that receives the maximum sunlight. In constant shade they become leggy and reluctant to flower. In autumn when they have finished flowering, the plants should be discarded and either burnt or composted.

Popular annuals and biennials include:

Alyssum. A low growing plant, up to 4in high, with white, mauve or pink flowers. Sow outdoors in April to May. Suitable to grow on a wall between stones, or as a rock plant as well as its more common use as an edging to beds and borders.

If you do not have adequate facilities for raising your own seedlings, buy young plants from a nursery instead.

Antirrhinum. The snapdragon that children love. A useful plant where height is needed, since it grows up to 30in tall, depending on variety. Flowers are red, orange, pink, yellow or white. Sow seed indoors from January to April for flowers from June to October.

Begonia semperflorens. The small, bedding begonia approximately 6in tall, with glossy leaves and tiny red, pink or white flowers. Useful for leaf colour and contrast; sow indoors in January to March for flowers from June to October.

► A striking short term effect; vibrant colour offsets the cool green of a lawn in summer.

▼ Annuals and biennials can be used to fill spaces in a shrub border and bring a splash of seasonal colour to beds without permanent plants.

Begonia planting in the foreground shows clearly that a mass of flowers of one variety has more impact than planting in ones and twos.

Calendula. Known as pot marigold, calendula grows to 18in high, and flowers are cream, yellow or orange. Sow outdoors in March to May for flowers from June to September.

Campanula (Canterbury bell). A biennial flower that should be sown outdoors in April to June and will flower from May to July the following year. Plants grow up to 30in tall with a mass of small, bell shaped flowers on each stem. Flowers are white, pink, blue and mauve.

Centaurea (cornflower). A hardy annual that is best sown outdoors in late August to early September for bloom the following June (can also be sown in April to May for bloom from June to September). Cornflowers are excellent for cutting, particularly the taller double varieties. Colours are blue, white and pink; tall varieties grow to 2ft high, dwarf to 9in.

Cheiranthus (wallflower). The warm, russet tones of this biennial are a familar combination with bulbs in spring. Sow seeds outdoors in May to July to flower the following spring and summer. Plants grow 8 to 15in tall.

Eschscholzia. Known as Californian poppies, the flowers are saucer shaped and come in brilliant reds, oranges and yellows. Plants grow to approximately 12in high. Suitable for sunny, dry positions and where the soil is sandy. Sow seeds outdoors in September or March to April. Cut flowers off when dead, or seeds will spread and produce self-sown seedlings over a large area.

Helichrysum. There are two useful varieties of helichrysum. One is an annual known as straw flower, that grows up to 30in high. Seeds should be sown indoors in March or can be sown in the garden in April in warmer parts of the country. Flowers are suitable for drying.

Helichrysum lanatum is, strictly speaking, a shrub but it will not last outdoors through the winter. It is usually sold as a 'silver leaf' bedding plant, and its soft, downy leaves make an excellent contrast for brightly coloured flowers. Stems grow to 18-24in long with a tendency to curve and trail slightly.

Iberis (candytuft). An easy annual to grow. Flowers are white or shades of pink and purple and plants grow to approximately 9in high. Sow seed outdoors from March to June for summer flowering or in early autumn to bloom in late spring.

Lathyrus odoratus (sweet pea). Flowers are fragrant, come in a wide range of colours and are excellent for cutting. Sow seed outdoors in February to March. Plants grow to 7 or 8ft tall and need support from canes, twine or twiggy sticks. Distance between plants 6in.

Lobelia. A very familiar plant for edging raised beds and borders, and in tubs, pots or hanging baskets. Plants have tiny white, blue or pinkish flowers, and trailing varieties are available. Sow seeds indoors January to April for flowers June to October.

Malcomia maritima (Virginian stock). Easy to grow for colour from spring to mid-autumn. Sow seeds outdoors in March and continue sowing right through to September for a succession of bloom. Useful to grow in crevices between paving stones. Plants grow to just 6in high.

Nicotiana. Tobacco plant is an extremely useful annual. Flowers are at their best in the evening and give off a delightful fragrance. Plant them near the house or patio to enjoy fully. A valuable plant, too, for cutting, particularly the variety with greenish yellow flowers. Sow seeds indoors in February to April for flowers July to September. Plants grow to approximately 3ft high.

Nigella. Known by the romantic name of love-in-a-mist, the soft blue flowers are surrounded by fine feathery leaves creating a hazy effect. Good for cut flowers. Sow seeds outdoors in March to April; plants grow 12-18in high.

Papaver (poppy). There are many varieties of poppy, but two most commonly grown are:

Iceland poppy: Sow seeds outdoors in May to June for flowers the following year. Good for cut flowers. Grows to approximately 2ft high.

Shirley poppy: Sow outdoors in March to May for flowers June to September.

Petunia. Brightly coloured, bell shaped flowers are useful for a mass of colour approximately 12in high, and for pots and window boxes. Full sun is essential. Sow seeds indoors in March to April for flowers June to October.

Salvia. Large, bright red, conical shaped flowers with a rather stiff appearance but excellent for a splash of colour. Grows 8-18in depending on variety. Sow indoors in February to March for flowers June to September.

Tagetes erecta (African marigold). Double flowers, yellow or orange, grow up to 3in in diameter on straight stems 15 to 20in high. The effect is reminiscent of lollipops. Sow indoors in February to March and plant out in late May to June or sow outdoors in May for flowers from June to September.

Tagetes patula (French marigold). A less formal plant with smaller, single or double orange or yellow flowers. Plants grow 8 to 12in high. Sow indoors in March to April or outdoors in May for flowers from June to September.

Tropaeolum majus (nasturtium). A familiar climbing or trailing plant with red, orange or yellow flowers; large leaves can be used in salad. Grows best in full sun in soil with little or no food. Sow seeds outdoors in April to May for flowers June to October. Heights vary according to variety from 9in to 6ft.

Bulbs

For most people the word bulb probably conjures up images of brightly coloured spring flowers — the familiar daffodils, tulips and so on. However, the word bulb is, in fact, a term that encompasses all bulbous plants sold in a dormant condition. As well as true bulbs, these include corms, tubers and rhizomes, which produce such flowers as gladioli, dahlias and flag irises respectively.

The shape and size may differ, but they all fulfil the same basic function — that of tiding the plant over adverse conditions such as winter cold or summer drought. In order to fulfil this function they share certain characteristics, including food storage, and quick growth under suitable conditions. Their life cycle, too, is the same; during growth and flowering the following year's flower is formed in miniature, so that when a bulb has finished flowering its leaves and roots simply die away.

This rather self-sufficient method of reproduction means that flowers from bulbs are easy to grow because their success is virtually guaranteed. You might say that commonsense plays a more important part than green fingers! As with other plants, bulbs should be planned as part of the overall garden scheme. Spring flowering bulbs are particularly useful in this

To grow half-hardy annuals from seed indoors, sow thinly in a pot or tray containing moistened seed sowing compost.

Cover with a layer of moist compost roughly equal in depth to the diameter of the seed (Tiny seeds like lobelia need no covering).

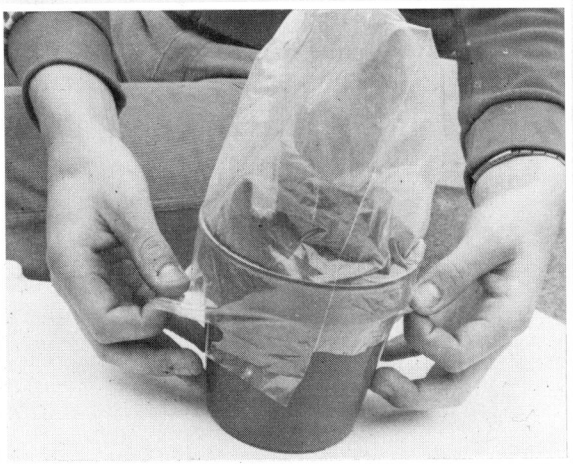

Cover with polythene and stand in a warm place until the seedlings germinate. Then uncover the pot and transfer it to a light position.

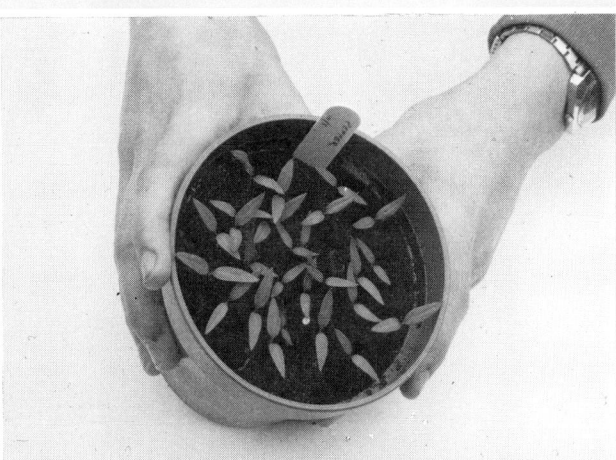

When the seedlings are large enough to handle they should be transplanted or pricked out.

Fill individual pots with potting compost and use a dibber to transplant one seedling to each pot, taking care not to damage the roots.

► Summer flowers are useful for instant effect in small spaces and containers. This planter would brighten any wall.

► Dianthus is just one of the many summer flowers that has a lovely perfume as well as an attractive appearance.

► Groups of annuals are arranged in a colour scheme of red, yellow and white. The red patio chairs add a stylish finishing touch.

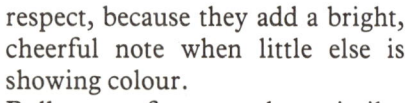

respect, because they add a bright, cheerful note when little else is showing colour.

Bulbs can, of course, play a similar role to annual summer flowers, filling in spaces in newly planted beds and borders. However, as with annuals, a riotous mixture of pink, yellow, blue and red can be somewhat overpowering in our opinion. A greater impact can be made by groups of one particular flower or a mixture of not more than two.

There are, in fact, bulb flowers to suit almost every purpose in the garden. Miniature spring flowering bulbs such as *Narcissus nana,*

▲
Bulbs are easy to grow and add cheer to a garden when little else is in colour.

Iris reticulata, snowdrops and muscari, are ideal for rock gardens. The charm of their tiny flowers is undeniable, and they are welcome as a seasonal addition to alpine plants, most of which flower in mid-summer. Moreover, there are varieties of crocus to flower during autumn, winter and spring. Plant the bulbs in pockets of peaty soil

59

between rocks, where they will spread and establish themselves, their delicate flowers forming a satisfying contrast to the solid feeling of the rock.

Narcissi (including daffodils) and crocus are particularly suited to planting in grass, where they will naturalize. This need not be restricted to the formal lawn area; indeed the effect is one of distinct informality. Naturalized bulbs are successful on a grassy slope or bank, in an area of longer, rough grass, beneath a solitary tree or large shrub which has interest for a limited period of the year, or in a woodland type of garden, with a number of established trees.

In order to achieve the desired effect of informality, it is essential to avoid planting bulbs in straight lines or geometric patterns. They should simply be scattered over the area and planted where they fall, provided that they are not so close to each other that their natural growth would be restricted. Once planted, the bulbs will take care of themselves, increasing naturally from year to year. As time goes by, you will probably notice that the flowers become slightly smaller and lighter in colour.

Growing flowers from bulbs is a fast way of achieving colour and interest. You can move into a new house in early autumn and have masses of bloom just a few months later. The temporary nature of the flowers allows for a breathing space meanwhile, and during this time the permanent layout of the garden can be planned. The bulbs can, of course, be planted again as part of the layout in the following autumn.

Buying and planting bulbs

When buying bulbs look for ones that are heavy for their size, plump and free from scars and firm to the touch. If they are not to be planted straightaway, open the bags for ventilation and store the bulbs in a cool, dry place.

Bulbs grow well in almost any soil that drains well, in sun or partial shade. If the soil in your garden is heavy, or clay, then add sand and peat to help drainage; if it is sandy, mix in a quantity of peat.

Planting time for bulbs varies. Daffodils can be planted in September, and not later than November. Tulips can be planted from October to the arrival of hard frosts, hyacinths from September to November and small bulbs like crocus and snowdrops between September and December.

Make a hole in the soil with a trowel, to the correct depth for the bulb being planted. This varies according to its size, and is approximately twice the depth of the bulb itself. Thus crocuses and snowdrops are set approximately 3in deep, hyacinths and daffodils 5-6in and tulips approximately 4in. A similar space should be allowed between bulbs.

Be sure to plant with the pointed end uppermost, cover with soil and gently firm. The soil should be kept slightly moist during the bulb's period of growth, and it may be necessary to water during dry weather, particularly bulbs in containers.

When the bulbs have flowered and the petals start to fade, remove the dead blooms but allow the leaves to die down naturally as they will replace the food store. If bulbs are planted in grass, the leaves should die down before the grass is cut.

Bulbs can be removed from the soil when the leaves have withered; they should be cleaned, and stored in a cool, airy place that is free from frost, and can be replanted the following autumn.

If the bulbs are left in the soil, they can increase quite quickly, and may become congested after three or four years. When this happens dig up the clump, divide the bulbs and replant the largest bulbs in fresh sites where a sprinkling of bonemeal has been forked into the soil.

Which bulbs to grow?

Everyone is familiar with daffodils, crocuses, tulips and hyacinths, but there are many more less common bulbs that are well worth growing.

Less usual autumn flowering bulbs include colchicum — similar to crocuses — and nerines, delicate members of the lily family. Winter and spring see the flowers of allium, the golden ornamental garlic; anemones and fritillaria — snake's head, which has intriguingly patterned, hood-like flowers.

Also worth growing are winter aconites, less usual species of narcissus, including *N. triandrus albus,* with flowers that almost resemble fragile birds in flight, and ornithogalum, the Star of Bethlehem.

Bulbs for cut flowers

Many bulb flowers are excellent for cutting. Naturalized bulbs can generally stand up to being raided with a pair of scissors. They grow in such profusion that the removal of a few blooms will not spoil the display, although the leaves should be cut as little as possible. This is also true of the miniature early flowering bulbs, such as snowdrops and muscari (grape hyacinth); both make charming table decorations.

However, it is a pity to spoil a natural outdoor display for the sake of enjoying the blooms for only a few days indoors. If you are keen to have plenty of cut flowers then, as for annuals, allocate a special part of the garden for the purpose. Summer flowering bulbs such as gladioli, freesias and dahlias can be grown with the summer annuals, since they must be lifted at the end of the growing season and replanted the following spring.

Spring flowers such as narcissus, tulips, lilies and Dutch iris can be grown in a permanent area. The taller flowers should be staked as they grow, to give support and encourage straight stems. Bent stems are a flower arrangers' nightmare!

Nearly all bulbs should be cut when the buds are just beginning to open, and the best time of day for cutting is early morning, when the dew is still on the flowers. After cutting place flowers in about three inches of tepid water in a clean bucket and leave for at least six hours in a cool, dark place. Narcissi should be kept separate, as these exude a milky liquid that affects the vase life of other bulb flowers.

Gardening in pots, tubs and containers

The enjoyment of spring bulb and summer annual flowers need not be restricted to garden beds and borders. Both are eminently suitable for growing in outdoor containers of many kinds. Plant bulbs in autumn for spring flowers, and when they have finished flowering plant annuals. In this way you will have almost non-stop colour all through spring, summer and early autumn.

For both bulbs and annuals, ensure that the pot, tub or box has a drainage hole in the bottom, and cover this with 'crocks' — pieces of a broken clay flower pot or a similar material — to prevent the hole from becoming clogged with soil. The pot should be almost filled with moist compost; use a proprietary lightweight compost for potting or John Innes No. 3. The lack of weight, if soilless composts are used, will facilitate moving pots around in the garden. Bulbs should be planted in the pot in the same way as in the garden, with the pointed end uppermost, but can be planted quite close together, provided that they are not touching each other or the sides of the pot. Gently firm the compost over the bulbs and water well. Water fairly regularly in dry weather and ensure that the compost does not dry out.

Bulbs in a container will not be damaged by the weather conditions of an average or mild British winter, but during very cold spells it is advisable to protect them by covering the pot with several thicknesses of newspaper or sacking.

Additional bulbs can be grown in ordinary flower pots sunk into soil in an odd corner of the garden. In spring these can be transplanted — keeping the soil and roots intact — into your decorative container to fill any gaps or give a succession of flowers.

When the bulbs have finished flowering, they can be lifted from the container and replanted in a corner of the garden to allow the leaves to die down naturally. This will leave the container free, so that it can be planted with annuals. If you buy these as bedding plants, in boxes, pots or trays, they can be planted directly into the container, firming the compost around them and watering well. As with bulbs, it is possible to position plants slightly closer than you would in the garden, to achieve a bushy display with maximum impact.

If you want to use flowers that you have grown from seed yourself, it is a good idea to sow the seed in the normal way, but transplant seedlings to grow on individually in small peat pots; these should be kept moist at all times. When the young plants have been hardened off, the peat pots can simply be planted into soil in the container, where they will eventually rot away, leaving the flowers to flourish.

The soil surface in a container is generally such a small area that a selection of one or two different plants is adequate. More would look too fussy and detract from the decorative use of the container and plants as a harmonising unit.

If you are selecting a combination of flowers, consider both shape and colour. Salvias could, for instance, be combined with *Helichrysum lanatum*. The upright red flowers are a pleasing contrast to the horizontal stems and silver leaves. Similarly, white petunias can be edged with dark blue lobelia.

Containers planted with bulbs are, in our opinion, most successful when devoted to a single type of plant. Even an old bucket can look attractive when it is topped by a mass of daffodils. Hyacinths are bold, distinctive flowers and are not always easy to fit into a garden planting scheme, but in a container they are ideal. They look perfect from any angle, need no staking and are heavily perfumed. Planting a single variety will ensure that all bulbs bloom simultaneously.

Selecting the container

If you have only a tiny garden or paved courtyard where there is little or no space for plant beds, then containers will be especially important as a means of bringing plant colour and interest. They are, of course, almost equally valuable in a larger garden since they add a decorative touch in many contexts.

Even if you have only one container it is possible to obtain a colourful display for most of the year.

However, as with the selection of other garden materials and accessories, they should be chosen to complement the style of the layout and the house itself, rather than presenting a contrast that jars.

The colour of terracotta pots gives them a warm appearance that can enhance both modern and older properties, particularly houses that are built in red brick, since the shade and texture will blend. Containers made from terracotta are available in a wide range of shapes and sizes, from the humble flowerpot to a large, bulbous form with ring handles attached. There are also pots to hang against a wall, bringing something of a Mediterranean feel.

► Many summer flowering bulbs, such as these striking lilies, are useful for cut flower arrangements.

▼ Gardening in containers: here they add interest to a patio, blending with the style and colour of the furniture.

Plants make all the difference! Window boxes and troughs are a simple way of brightening up an otherwise dull block of flats.

Terracotta allows the roots of plants to breathe, but the soil will dry out more quickly than in containers made from a less porous material.

Concrete or reconstructed stone containers are often made in traditional shapes that would not look out of place in a stately period home. They are, therefore, not easy to blend with the garden of a small, modern house since both size and style are inappropriate.

They can, however, be more suitable for a Victorian house or even a newer house built in the 'Georgian' style that has become popular during recent years.

Containers made from lightweight asbestos or fibreglass cement are, on the other hand, more modern in appearance. Many have a simple, architectural form such as a basic square or cylinder and are ideally suited to a newer property, although care should be taken not

to select a very large pot for a very small garden. A shallow, rectangular container can be used to make a sink garden with alpine plants, small rocks and pebbles. This will thrive in a sunny position.

Plastic, too, is a modern material and is often more successful in simple forms than as a copy of a typical traditional urn. Plastic is generally lightweight, both in feel and appearance, and it is therefore wise to avoid planting a container with a heavy, bushy shrub. Smaller plants with a slightly more fragile form look better and are more practical.

Timber is expensive nowadays, but wooden tubs and boxes are hard to beat for planting with a shrub or small tree. They are not only substantial, but look sufficiently solid to balance the appearance of the heavier plant.

The types of containers mentioned by no means represent all the possibilities for objects that will hold plants. It can be fun to innovate, using an old barrel sawn in half, or almost any clean, sound container that can be left outdoors and has holes drilled in the bottom.

Pots made from ceramic material and some types of plastic may be susceptible to damage from frost and cold temperatures. They can therefore be planted with subjects such as fatsia or a bay tree, which can be left outside during the summer and taken into a porch or hallway for the winter months.

Hanging pots and baskets

A hanging basket can brighten up any view that lacks eye-level interest. Hang one outside the kitchen window, on a bracket attached to the wall, from the roof of a porch or even a car port.

Baskets are generally available in either solid plastic or wire mesh. The solid type can simply be filled with compost, but it is necessary to line a mesh basket with moss. Recent years have seen the introduction of self-watering hanging pots, which slowly take up water from their own reservoir and simply need topping up from time to time. However, few of these will stand up to cold weather and should therefore be used outdoors only in summer.

Suitable plants for hanging pots and baskets include ivy-leafed geraniums and hanging fuchsias; these can be edged with trailing lobelia.

Permanent plants for containers

We have discussed at some length the use of plants of a temporary nature for pots, tubs and other decorative containers. However, there are also many permanent shrubs and even trees that can be successfully grown in this way.

Particularly valuable are plants that have attractive qualities as an individual specimen, and something of interest to be seen all round. There are suitable dwarf and low growing conifers that will retain their shape in a restricted space for many years. However, we like to experiment a little with beautifully shaped plants that might normally grow to a larger size.

A young specimen of *Cedrus atlantica glauca,* which normally grows as an upright plant with narrow branches, was spotted growing unstaked as a container plant in a garden centre; it had assumed a slight lean that was rather appealing. It was planted in a decorative container of about 3ft diameter and 12in in height, and was regularly fed. In spring some of the new growth was cut back to restrict the plant's size; the process resembles somewhat the Japanese craft of Bonsai. The plant formed an attractive, established feature and will continue to do so for many years. Ultimately such a shrub, if not cared for, would become rather large and could then be transplanted into the garden, where it would in time grow on to its normal, unrestricted size.

Both *Phormium tenax,* the New Zealand flax, and *Yucca filamentosa* have long, spiky leaves and their striking outline makes them ideal for a container, especially one with a narrow neck and wider body, since this echoes the shape of the plant and creates a feeling of balance. However, one

Container planting is not limited to annuals; certain forms of trees, shrubs and conifers can also be grown in suitable pots.

point to bear in mind is that once a permanent shrub has established its root system in a container with a narrow neck, it will be virtually impossible to remove without causing damage to the plant or effecting the destruction of the pot. A small, slow growing tree is a good choice for a container that is large and heavy. Most suitable perhaps are acers; their leaves are delicately feathery, in shades ranging from yellowish green to deep, russet reds, and the trunk can become twisted and full of character. A small, weeping, flowering cherry is another good choice, and its trunk can be underplanted with small bulbs for added interest.

When you buy a tree or shrub from a nursery or garden centre, it will probably be growing in a poly-thene or fibre pot. When you are ready to transplant it to your decorative container water the plant well and allow to drain. Meanwhile put crocks over the container's drainage hole and a layer of compost in the bottom. Remove the plant from its own container by carefully making one vertical slit in the side and one around the circumference of the base. The container can easily be pulled away, leaving the roots and soil intact.

Place the plant, with roots and soil, in the container and fill with moist compost so that the base of the stem or trunk is just 1½-2in below the rim of the container. Gently firm compost and water well.

The soil in a container will obviously dry out more quickly than that in a garden bed. Containers therefore need regular watering. It is impossible to dictate the frequency, since water should be given when the soil begins to feel dry, and the speed of this will depend on weather conditions and the material of the container.

Water liberally, so that the water drains freely from the base of the container, and feed plants with a general purpose liquid fertiliser. This should be diluted according to the instructions on the bottle and given at weekly intervals from April to October.

Positioning containers in the garden

A patio is often the flattest and most open part of the garden, and yet it is also most often the feature that presents an immediate view from the house. Planted containers are therefore ideal for introducing height and interest on the patio, close to the house windows. They also create a more pleasant atmos-phere for relaxing and soften a hard surface.

Containers can effectively be placed in groups of two or three to create a greater impact, but ensure that the plants will also look better together than individually. If all three are planted with different plants, they will appear to have been grouped together by accident rather than design and the object will have been defeated.

It is also a good idea to move pots and tubs to create a change of scene or to enjoy them at their best. For the handyman this can be made easier by the construction of a simple timber base with castors, upon which the container is positioned.

The front of the house should not be neglected. A planted tub by the front door adds a touch of style to the entrance, and gives a welcoming feel, assuming, of course, that there is adequate space. Your guests will not feel welcome if they fall over a pot getting to the front door!

Alternative forms of garden decoration

Planted pots are just one form of decoration in the garden, but are by no means the only way of adding the vital, personal touches to your layout. Indeed, a pot can sometimes be so attractive that it is worthy of consideration as an orna-ment in its own right, and plants seem superfluous. This is particularly true of containers with a distinctive shape, such as a terracotta 'Ali Baba' pot or an elaborate stone urn. Position them as a focal point in the design, or consider partially concealing them in a plant bed, to create an element of surprise.

A statue can equally be seen either as an object that arrests the eye,

A plant grown long-term in a container requires an adequate quantity of compost, regular watering and feeding to remain healthy.

being displayed in a prominent position, or one that is combined with plants. Part of its appeal in this context will be the contrast between living plants and a solid, inanimate object.

Many garden centres sell mass-produced stone figures as garden ornaments. If one seems right for the layout you have planned, then by all means introduce it as an attractive feature. However, if you would prefer something unique and individual, it may be worth approaching a local art school to see whether any of the students' work appeals.

If your taste indoors is for older furniture, then you may be attracted by an object in an antique or 'junk' shop that could, with imagination, be put to good use as a garden ornament. A cartwheel is a possibility, or even an old chimney pot.

Decoration of a flat area of paving need not take the form of either a pot or a statue. By simply varying the surface material and texture a decorative contrast can be achieved. Leave out just two or three slabs, and in their place position a piece of rock surrounded by shingle or large cobbles. Consider practicalities at the same time, for young children in the family will almost inevitably run or fall over such an interruption if they use the patio for playing.

It may be safer — and equally attractive — to break the appearance of the paving by planting areas of ground cover plants, such as camomile or thyme. These will not take regular foot traffic, but can be walked over occasionally, and both give off a pleasant aroma.

◄
The sculptural qualities of both plant and urn combine to form a dramatic focal point.

◄
A stylish little stone bird perched on a rock brings an element of decoration and almost surprise to a planted area.

A solid stone ornament is cleverly combined with plants so that its shape and texture become integral parts of the natural arrangement.

Rock and water features

The decorative features of a garden are just as important as its more practical aspects. They lend character and individuality to a layout, and represent an equally sound investment. After all, there are some months of the year when the weather prevents you from making a great deal of use of your outdoor living space. Certainly you can enjoy pursuing the activities of gardening, but you really appreciate having something that is good to look at as you sit in the protection of a warm living room. When the weather does improve, the existence of features such as a pool or rock garden encourages you to go out into the garden and enjoy them at close quarters.

Moreover, if you plan such features in your front garden, they will give pleasure not only to your own family, but to a lot of people who regularly walk — or drive — past your house. We always notice gardens that are attractive and well laid out, and they never cease to give great enjoyment in their own way.

Rock gardens

One of the most traditional ways of introducing a decorative feature is in the form of a rock garden. Few people with an average family garden have either the money, space or inclination to build a massive, grand scale rock bank complete with streams and waterfalls, but it is possible to create something equally effective in a small space.

We have all seen rock gardens that don't work — lumps of concrete dotted about uncomfortably on a mound of earth and weeds. They are best forgotten if you are anxious to find the best way of using rock in your own garden to its full advantage. Remember rather that your pattern should come from stone formations in their natural state. Most of us, while on holiday in the Lake District, Scotland, North Wales or many other parts of Great Britain, have visited beauty spots where rock — and perhaps water — are an essential part of the landscape.

Whether the rock has been beaten to a rugged face or worn pebble smooth by the elements, its appeal seems to lie in the feeling of solidity and permanence that it evokes. It has probably been there for thousands of years. This feeling is one that should be recreated in your garden, and will help to give it an established look.

The appearance of rock in its natural setting can give you further guidelines. Look at the size of the rock pieces; they vary enormously from large chunks to tiny pebbles, and the rock you use should do the same. 1-1½ tons should be a sufficient quantity of rock for a small feature, and the pieces should vary in size from, say, 2 to 3cwt to pebbles. However, the majority should, of course, be made up of pieces of a reasonable size in order to create an impact.

You will notice too that the strata of rock is often visible, and that it naturally follows the horizontal line of the earth's surface. The rock in your garden will look uncomfortably unnatural if you distort the strata line to any great extent, although it can be effective to tilt just one or two stones slightly. If the rock you use comes from moorland rather than a quarry, it will have a weathered face that has been exposed to the elements. This is the face that you want to see in your garden; it will help to give that feeling of a permanent and an established feature.

Having gained an impression of the general desired effect, the decision must be taken as to where your rock garden should be situated. The ideal site is a sunny, gently sloping bank where the soil

When buying rock for garden use think big — a number of small pieces together will lack impact.

is not too heavy and there are no large tree roots.

However, if your garden is flat, you can create an artificial bank, which may need to be supported by a retaining wall at the rear. Try to integrate the rock feature into its surroundings if you do this, so that the bank slopes gently to merge with the flatter ground around it rather than simply coming to an abrupt end.

Having decided on the site, you will want to turn your thoughts to selecting the type of rock to use. Prices can vary, and tend to depend a great deal on the transportation costs. It will, therefore, be cheaper to use a rock that is local to your area; there are attractive stones in many parts of the country.

The most familiar is probably the craggy, grey Westmorland rock, which in the south of England is very expensive. A better choice here might be Kent ragstone, with a brownish-buff colour that is easy to blend into almost any garden scheme.

Wherever you live, enquire at your local garden centres and stone merchants and go and look at the rock before you buy. You may even be able to choose exactly the pieces you would like. These will then be weighed, priced and delivered.

Newly quarried rock is often covered in a powdery slurry, but this cleans quite easily if the stone is hosed down.

When it comes to building your rock feature, ensure first that the site is clear of weeds and brickbats. Moving the rock is a job for two people, and pieces can be rolled or levered into position. Keep the site uncluttered and work tidily to avoid accidents. You only have to step back and trip over a large, craggy stone to sustain quite an unpleasant fall.

Start placing the rock at the bottom of the bank, using a large piece as a solid keystone. Build up in, say, three irregular steps to achieve both height and depth. The stones should be bedded securely into the bank, and not perch, wobbling on an edge. If they tilt back slightly a more natural effect will be achieved. The object to bear in mind is that the rock should appear to be the visible part of a much larger underground formation, and should almost seem to 'grow' out of its surroundings.

Use the variety of sizes to form outcrops on the edge of your feature, so that the rock is not all clustered in an isolated lump, but blends and fades gradually into the remainder of the garden.

As you position the rock, you will form pockets and cavities between stones. These provide the perfect environment for many small rock and alpine plants, but you should assist by providing a suitable soil.

Fill the plant pockets with a mixture of compost and a small quantity of sand. Good drainage is necessary for rock plants and so if the soil in your garden tends to be very heavy, add a little grit or shingle to assist drainage.

Some of the more familiar alpine and rock plants

Most thrive in well drained soil and require a sunny position. They are perennials, and so can be left in the ground to flower every year.

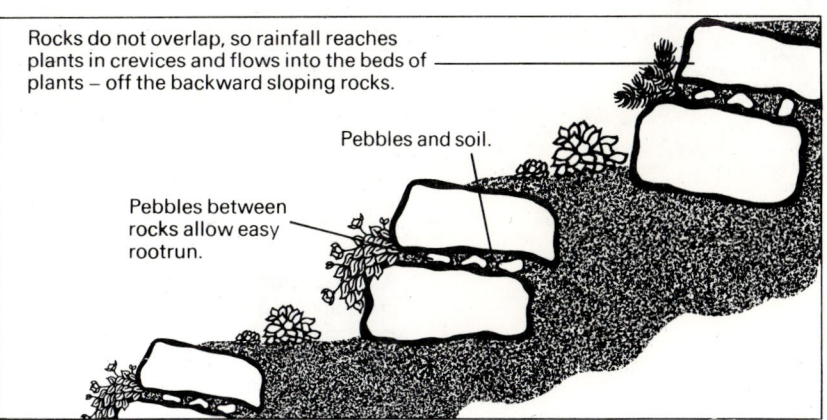

Rocks do not overlap, so rainfall reaches plants in crevices and flows into the beds of plants – off the backward sloping rocks.

Pebbles and soil.

Pebbles between rocks allow easy rootrun.

A well planned and constructed rock and water feature. Stone is set into the bank in groupings and outcrops that give a natural appearance; waterfalls add interest and movement, and planting helps to blend the feature with its surroundings.

Alpine plants, with their mass of tiny leaves and delicate flowers, fill cracks and crevices and contrast with the solidity of rock.

Miniature varieties of familiar shrubs, such as rhododendron, are excellent companions to rock, providing year-round interest and colour in spring and early summer.

Acaena. An evergreen with bronze tinged leaves — a spreading plant. *Acaena microphylla* makes a dense carpet.

Achillea. Yarrow has delicate stems and flattish flower heads, yellow or white, in July to August. The leaves have a pungent smell.

Alyssum saxatile. This perennial version of the familiar white annual flower has silver foliage and a mass of yellow flowers, which appear in spring.

Anemone x hybrida. A hybrid of the garden flower, known as the Japanese anemone. Flowers, white or pink, appear in late summer — early autumn.

Aubrieta. A favourite garden plant that has a lovely show of tiny blue, pink or mauve flowers in spring.

Campanula. Beautiful miniature bell flowers are in bloom in July to August, and are white, pink or mauve.

Dianthus. Pinks have sweetly scented flowers from June onwards in a wide range of colours.

Gentiana. The brilliant blue flower that is associated with the Swiss alps. Flowers in summer.

Helianthemum. Better known as rock rose; the plant grows quickly and a mass of pink, red, orange or yellow flowers bloom throughout the summer.

Iberis. Candytuft is an evergreen plant with dark green leaves and a mass of white flowers in early summer.

Phlox. The alpine varieties have great appeal, with tiny flowers in a range of pastel and brightly coloured shades. Flowers appear from June onwards.

Primula. Some varieties are suited to open positions and others prefer a damp, shady spot. A wonderful range of colours.

Saxifraga. There are many forms of the dainty saxifrage suitable for the rock garden, and probably one for just about every position and taste.

Sedum. Again a wide variety. Known as stonecrop, the plants form a dense cushion of succulent leaves and flower in late summer to early autumn.

Sempervivum. The houseleek too has succulent leaves in the form of rosettes. These alone are attractive, being of many different colours, and in addition the plant has flowers that bloom above the dense mass of the plant.

Thymus. Thyme has a mass of tiny evergreen leaves with a subtle aroma, particularly in full sunlight. The golden leafed, lemon scented variety is worth looking out for.

Viola. The lovely little creeping plant. Many varieties flower all through the summer.

Although many of these plants are evergreen, and most have brilliant flowers, they are at their best for a comparatively short time of the year. It is, therefore, a good idea to plant a framework of shrubs that will give permanent height and character to your rock feature, particularly as an interesting background.

Suitable background plants are those which have an interesting shape or colouring, such as *Acer palmatum* 'Dissectum'. This is a form of the Japanese maple which has finely cut, fresh green leaves that turn a bronze shade in autumn; equally attractive is *Acer palmatum* 'Dissectum Atropurpureum', a form with rich, reddish purple leaves.

Low growing shrubs with a spreading habit can be grown among the rocks. Suitable plants include hebe, the evergreen shrub also known as veronica, in particular *Hebe* 'Carl Teschner', with violet flowers and *Hebe pinguifolia* 'Pagei', with bluish leaves and white flower spikes. *Cytisus x beanii,* a low growing form of broom and *Genista hispanica* (Spanish gorse) are also suitable, as are the varieties of *Potentilla fruticosa.* Miniature forms of larger shrubs can be interesting additions to the rock garden; a particularly charming plant is *Rhododendron impeditum,* which grows to just about 10 to 12in in height.

Conifers and rock are, of course, a familiar combination. Varieties that grow slowly to reach a fair size are good as background planting. These include *Juniperus scopulorum* 'Skyrocket', a dramatic, pencil shaped plant, as the name suggests, and *Chamaecyparis lawsoniana* 'Ellwoodii'. This plant has dark

green foliage, and 'Ellwood's Gold' is a striking yellow colour.

For planting in the rock garden itself, it is advisable to choose dwarf or slow growing conifers, as these will never grow so large as to be out of scale and proportion. *Picea glauca* 'Albertiana Conica' may have a large name, but the plant grows to just 3ft tall, and takes many years to do so. It has a cone-like shape hence the term 'conica' in its name.

Chamaecyparis obtusa 'Nana Gracilis' is another good dwarf with rich green foliage arranged in small sprays. For constant golden colour *Chamaecyparis lawsoniana* 'Minima Aurea' is an excellent choice, and is very slow growing, attaining only about 2ft in height in ten years.

When looking for dwarf conifers in a garden centre, do not be tempted to buy plants that simply look small, and are growing in small pots. They may well be very young specimens of much faster growing plants, and it is always advisable to check with a knowledgeable plantsman to ensure that you obtain slow growing specimens suitable for a rock garden.

It is, perhaps, impossible to consider conifers for the rock garden without thinking of heathers, for the two are a natural combination. Most heathers will not grow in limy or chalky soil, particularly the summer flowering varieties. However, *Erica carnea* varieties and *Erica darleyensis* are exceptions, and are valuable additions to any garden.

The great advantage of ericas and callunas, which together form the range of heaths and heathers, is that there is a variety to flower at every time of year. This means that by choosing carefully you could have year-round colour. However, it is advisable to avoid planting, say, one plant each of ten varieties, for the effect will be patchy, and the plants will have little impact. It is better to narrow your choice to, say, three groups of three plants, with colours of flower and foliage that will blend and not clash.

It is worth bearing in mind the fact that although a rock feature involves quite an investment initially, in terms of both money and effort, it can prove very worthwhile in the long term. If you choose conifers, ericas and other shrubs they will require little maintenance once established. If you decide to experiment with flowering rock and alpine plants, their collection and care can become a fascinating hobby. One thing is certain; whatever your aim in creating a rock garden, if you build with care, thought and a touch of artistic flair, the result will be a feature of lasting and increasing beauty.

Pools and water features

We have mentioned the fact that many of the most beautiful natural rock landscapes have water as an essential part of their formation. Water is always fascinating, whether it takes the form of a rushing, tumbling waterfall or a still, calm lake. It can both soothe and excite the senses, and tempts people to just stand and gaze.

The most obvious way of introducing water to your garden is in the form of a simple pool. Perhaps the most desirable position for the pool is as a feature of the patio, where you can see and enjoy it whilst relaxing outdoors or when sitting or working inside the house. If you decide to plan a pool as a feature of the lawn area, try to ensure that it forms an integral part of the design, and does not suddenly appear for no particular reason.

However, if the only suitable position for a pool is some distance from the house, this can have the advantage of encouraging people to go right into the garden, as they will naturally be drawn to the water.

The site for a pool should be in sunlight for at least half the day, and preferably the whole day. It should also be level and away from the overhanging branches of trees, for falling leaves will pollute the water and make a mess that is almost impossible to clear.

Having planned your site, it will be necessary to consider the shape of the pool, and this should be determined by the line and style of the garden layout. A formal town

The choice of conifers for a rock garden is crucial — seek advice and avoid planting over-vigorous varieties.

Rock plants with flower and foliage interest combine to make an impressive show in a mature garden, clothing the stone and softening its appearance.

A sink garden can be the answer for those with an interest in rock gardening but a strictly limited space, and can add real charm to a patio.

▲
A stunning specimen of Japanese azalea;
the scale, shape and size of the plant are in
keeping with a rock setting.

►
Rock placed dramatically on a sloping
bank planted with miniature conifers and
heathers.

garden would be the appropriate setting for a regular square, or rectangular pool, or a variation of these such as an L-shape or rectangle with curved, Roman-style ends.

However, if you want to combine your pool with a rock feature, building in a stream or waterfall, it should always be an informal, free-form shape. Curves should be bold and sweeping rather than forming intricate nooks and crannies. This not only looks better, but is more practical for the pool construction.

A depth of 18in will create a pool that provides a suitable environment for fish and water plants, but it is preferable to allow a 9in wide shelf around the inside perimeter, at a depth of 9in. This provides a position for marginal plants. The sides of the pool should slope slightly inwards.

Perhaps the simplest method of making a garden pool is the installation of a plastic pool liner. Liners are available in varying grades and forms of plastic material, including basic polythene, PVC or tough butyl, a synthetic rubber. Cost, durability and life of the pool will obviously depend on the quality of material you use.

The liner should be sufficiently large to fit the pool shape with a good overlap all round. Installation simply involves marking out and digging a hole of the required shape and size, and picking out any stones from the soil. The shaped soil should then be covered with a layer of sand.

Spread the liner over the pool shape and secure temporarily at the edges, using stones or small slabs, then start to fill with water (ordinary tap water is quite satisfactory). As the pool fills the liner should be allowed to ease in to fit tightly the excavated shape. It will be necessary to adjust the weights around the edges for this purpose. When the pool is full of water, trim any excess plastic so that there is an overlap of approximately 4in all round. The pool surround can then be paved, or disguised with rock stone where appropriate.

A more expensive form of pool construction is the installation of a pre-formed pool shape. These are made from rigid fibreglass or a more flexible plastic material. A good range of informal shapes is generally available, particularly from water garden specialists.

The construction process is similar to that of a plastic liner pool, in that it is necessary to excavate a hole of the appropriate size and shape and line it with sand. The pool 'mould' can then be placed in the ground and filled with water, and the soil tidied and flattened around it. The pool edges should be disguised with paving or any suitable form of ground surfacing, in the same way as for the liner pool.

The construction of a concrete pool is a more complicated process. A hole should be dug to the required shape, as with the other methods, and this forms the basis for a floor and walls constructed from a 6in depth of concrete. The concrete mix usually consists of a combination of ¾in ballast and cement, together with a small quantity of waterproofing powder, which helps to counter the rather porous nature of the material. When the concrete shell is set, it is coated with a cement mortar render to a thickness of about ½in. The entire process is best carried out in summer months, during dry weather.

The final stage of construction is the application of a sealing compound to neutralise the free lime in the concrete; this is most important for the survival of fish. If you contemplate the construction of a concrete pool, obtain as much detailed information as possible before you commence work.

A raised pool

Of course, a pool does not have to be at ground level. If yours is intended as a feature of the patio, why not raise the finished level to a height of, say, 2ft. It is pleasant and cooling on a hot day to have water close by, and almost everyone — particularly children — will be unable to resist the temptation to dabble their hand in the water. Where children are concerned, a raised pool can be considerably safer, for there is less danger of

Water in a garden holds a great fascination for children — a raised pool can be safer.

them falling whilst peering into the water.

The construction need not be complicated, and a plastic liner can be used. Build up two or three courses of brickwork using either ordinary clay bricks or a decorative manufactured block. Fit the liner in the pool shape, and secure the overlap by fixing a row of bricks, laid side by side rather than end to end, or a manufactured coping stone. One or two manufacturers of paving and walling products market a raised pool in kit form, and this can be more straight-forward for the less confident do-it-yourselfer.

Having tackled the basic pool construction, you will want to turn your thoughts to the finishing touches that will create a worth-while water feature, and a really decorative asset to your garden.

Water plants

Water plants are one important aspect of these finer points, but you should allow the water in a new pool to settle for a few days before introducing plants.

When it comes to choosing the plants, you should go to a garden centre with a good aquatic depart-ment or to a water garden specialist, who may also sell by mail order. Such companies often offer a collection of plants, and this assists in ensuring a balanced environment in the pool.

You will probably find that the plants are sold planted in small, plastic mesh baskets. These can be placed directly in the pool, and the plants will remain in them and become established. This method eliminates the need for a layer of soil in the base of the pool. The best time to plant is from June to September.

There are plants to fulfil various purposes in the pool, and each should be allocated its proper position.

Marginal plants growing in the plastic baskets should be positioned on the shelf around the edge of the pool. These will, in fact, grow in either wet soil or water up to about 6in deep. Plants include marsh marigold, cotton grass, which grows 12in high and

is topped by fluffy white tufts, many moisture loving varieties of iris and *Lobelia cardinalis,* a striking plant with bright red flowers on stems about 2ft tall. Deep marginal plants are totally submerged in their baskets, and include the water violet, with its mass of lavender coloured flowers.

Water lilies are probably the most familiar of aquatic plants, but they should be placed sparingly in the pool, as each plant requires approximately 25 sq. ft of water surface. Plants should be placed in their basket on bricks initially, and gradually lowered as they mature and the stems grow longer. A wealth of beautiful flower colours are available. 'Alba' is a favourite white variety and 'Rose Arey' has delightful, deep pink, scented flowers. Of the red flowering varieties 'Escarboucle' is superb, and 'Sunrise' has large, golden yellow blooms.

Floating plants are placed on the water surface. Among more common types are the various forms of duckweed, but for something unusual the water lettuce *(Pistia stratoites)* has great appeal. The plant resembles a lettuce with thick, attractively shaped leaves, but it is not hardy and should be kept indoors during winter months.

The final, and perhaps most important, group of plants is the oxygenating plants. These are the forms of 'water weed' that ensure clean, algae-free water, and are an essential feature of any garden pool. The plants can be bought in bunches, and the stems should be pressed into soil in a basket. They will soon take root and become established of their own accord.

Fish for your pool

A selection of water plants will help to create the right conditions in the pool for ornamental fish. Goldfish are the most common choice, but there are many other types that will live in coldwater pools. These include Shubunkins, which may have a mixture of red, yellow, blue, brown or even violet coloured scales. Golden Orfe swim near the water surface so that they can clearly be seen in summer

Buy water plants from a specialist who will advise on the most appropriate plants for your size of pool.

Water is always fascinating. A still, calm lake has a tranquil, soothing effect that tempts people to just stand and gaze.

An informal pool with rock feature; the somewhat harsh line of the edge is broken by waterside planting.

Hostas are superb foliage plants for the waterside or any damp, shady position in the garden. Useful, too, for the flower arranger.

months, and a more recent introduction is the Japanese Koi carp, a beautiful fish that can grow to a large size, and is therefore better suited to the larger pool.

As a general rule, you should allow a 2in length of fish to every square foot of water surface in a new pool, and they can be introduced to the pool about two weeks after the installation of plants. The fish should be fed for the first few months with a proprietary fish food, and thereafter feeding during autumn and spring only should be sufficient.

It is surprising how tame fish can become, particularly if they are fed regularly at the same time every day, when they may even become sufficiently bold to eat out of your hand.

If they are given the right pool conditions, fish will generally remain quite healthy. However, they are unfortunately susceptible to a number of diseases if the water is polluted by surplus uneaten food, decaying leaves or even garden chemicals. It is therefore important to avoid both pollution of water and simply putting more fish into your pool than the volume of water will support.

An additional safeguard is to purchase your fish from a reputable supplier, so that they do not introduce disease from the outset. Furthermore, the introduction of molluscs, or water snails, will also be of benefit in keeping the pool water free from decaying matter.

Fountains and waterfalls

Moving water is always fascinating; it looks refreshing and the sound has immense appeal. A fountain can make an attractive focal point. Whilst there is no scope in the average garden for an impressive column of moving water along the lines of the famous landmarks of Versailles or even Trafalgar Square, it is not difficult to install a modest fountain that will give equal pleasure on a somewhat smaller scale.

The most common misconception regarding fountains is that a constant supply of running water must be on hand. In fact, all that is needed is an electric submersible pump to circulate the water. The principle is quite simple. A lead is plugged in to an ordinary earthed three-pin socket indoors in a position convenient for access to the garden. An extension cable leads into the garden via a transformer, which reduces voltage to a low level for safety. In the garden the cable is joined by a weatherproof connector to a sealed electric cable. This cable is connected to a small pump, which operates silently, completely submerged under the pool water.

The weatherproof connector can be covered with a piece of timber or a small paving slab, to enable easy access should the pump have to be disconnected, thus avoiding the need to disturb the extension cable.

A fountain attachment is fixed on top of the pump, and will create a jet of water — usually adjustable in height — by circulating the water in the pool. No other water supply is needed, although during hot weather you may find that it is necessary to top up the pool to compensate for the slight volume of water lost through evaporation.

If you have a very small patio pool, a fountain may cause problems when there is a breeze, since the water will be borne by the breeze and may splash beyond the confines of the pool itself. The answer here is a small bubble fountain, which takes the form of a low globe of water safely confined within the pool.

A further possibility for a restricted space is the installation of a gargoyle fountain. A raised pool should be constructed immediately in front of a vertical wall, into which a gargoyle 'mask' is built. Many garden and aquatic centres sell these in the form of a lion's head or dolphin spout. The submersible circulating pump is positioned in the pool and is fitted not with a fountain attachment, but with a length of plastic tubing which leads to the gargoyle spout, and is built in to the wall. The pump then circulates the pool water through the gargoyle fountain, creating an attractive feature at eye level.

A fountain is not the only feature

Who can resist moving water in a garden? Even the smallest area can accommodate a fountain.

that can be created by the use of a submersible pump. A waterfall is a more ambitious project, but its appeal springs from the natural and irresistible movement of sparkling water dancing and splashing over solid rock stones.

A waterfall or stream should be integrated with a pool, and should be constructed so that the water springs — apparently from a rock — at a point some three to five feet higher than the pool itself.

It is possible to use a pre-formed fibreglass waterfall chute, but these do tend to have a rather rigid and unnatural appearance. A more flexible design can be achieved by the use of a plastic liner or even a concrete base. A submersible pump is once again used to circulate the water from the pool, through plastic piping to the head of the waterfall; this is buried just beneath the surface of the soil beside the stream.

There are several design points to consider when planning the course of your waterfall, and the positioning of rock. Firstly, the path should not follow a straight line, either vertically or horizontally. Stagger the fall in steps, and stagger the path so that it appears to meander through its surroundings.

Choose carefully the stone over which the water finally falls into the pool. A large, dished stone 2 to 3in thick is ideal, and this should overhang the edge of the pool. If the edge of the stone itself is smooth, a level sheet of water will cascade from it, but if the edge is grooved and irregular, the water will bounce and splash as it falls, creating a more informal effect. The path of the water can be broken by small pieces of rock and large pebbles, so that it tumbles and splashes off them.

The sound of the waterfall will probably have as much appeal as its appearance, and this is governed by the depth in the pool. Shallow water will produce a light, tinkling sound and deep water a deeper, more resonant tone. If there are fish in the pool, ensure that they have sufficient space away from the moving and white water.

Plants for the waterside and damp positions

If your garden has no open area that is suitable for a pool, it is possible to grow moisture-loving plants in a damp and partially shaded position. They would be equally suited to the damp ground beside a pool or stream. Their flowers and foliage will soften the pool surround and their reflection in the water of the pool will add an extra dimension to its beauty.

Some of the most suitable plants include:

Astilbe. Flowers are delicate, feathery plumes on long, slender stems 2-3ft tall, and appear in summer. Colours are red, pink and white.

Astilbe chinensis is a miniature variety, just 8 to 12in tall, with deep purplish pink flowers.

Gunnera manicata. A magnificent plant with vast, flat leaves similar to those of rhubarb. Strictly for large gardens, as a specimen can grow to a massive size, often approaching 10 or 12ft across.

Hosta. A superb plant that thrives in any damp, shady position in the garden. The leaves are the main feature of interest, being large and flat and excellent for flower arranging. There are many varieties, perhaps the most familiar being *Hosta fortunei*, with delicate green leaves, and *Hosta sieboldiana*, with darker, bluish green leaves with a deeply ridged surface.

Iris sibirica. This herbaceous form of iris grows to a large clump of narrow foliage with white, blue or purplish flowers, 2 to 3ft high. Flowers appear in summer.

Primula. There are several moisture loving types of primula suitable for the edge of the pool. Perhaps the most notable forms are *Primula denticulata*, with beautiful round flower heads, mauve or white, and *Primula florindae*, with yellow flowers on long stems 2 to 3ft high, and foliage with the subtle aroma of cloves.

Rheum palmatum 'Rubrum'. A plant with large, reddish leaves of real architectural value. It should be grown individually as a specimen where space permits, since it can grow to 4 or 5ft high.

For the ambitious gardener the construction of a waterfall will present a real challenge and intrigue the neighbours!

A series of fountains makes an attractive focal point in a stream. The moving water adds life to a scene that is already bursting with vibrant spring colour.

▶

The finely cut leaves of *Acer palmatum* 'Dissectum Atropurpureum' are ideal for overhanging the water's edge.

Water plants add the finishing touches to a garden pool; they also help to keep the water clean and create a balanced environment for ornamental fish.

▶ Reflection of waterside plants adds an extra dimension to the beauty of a pool. The soft colour and weeping shape of a laburnum in flower make it an ideal choice. But beware of planting where children play as seeds are poisonous.

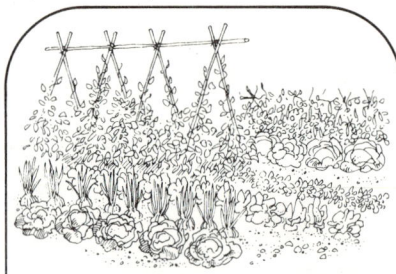

Growing vegetables

The idea of sitting down to a family meal consisting of vegetables freshly picked from your own garden is immensely satisfying. In order to do so, it is not necessary to devote the entire plot to vegetable production, nor do you need to become a total 'self sufficiency' devotee, complete with chickens at the end of the garden and a goat tethered to the fence! For the family with an average size garden it is better to aim to supplement your diet, rather than to totally replace produce bought from the greengrocer.

The prices of vegetables in the shops have varied enormously over the last two or three years, and if you decide to grow your own with the sole aim of saving a lot of money on the housekeeping, then you may be disappointed, although you will almost certainly make some savings on shop prices. This is particularly true if you plan to grow vegetables that are only occasionally available in the shops, and always at fairly high prices, such as broccoli, sweet corn, fresh peas or even asparagus.

Probably greater than the financial reward will be the pleasure of eating food that is freshly picked or pulled, as a result of your own efforts — and, as we have said, the sense of satisfaction it brings. You can gain a real feeling of achievement at having fulfilled the traditional instinct of 'working the land'. Home-grown vegetables also taste better, and you can grow varieties that are selected for their flavour, and are not often grown commercially.

When you set out to grow vegetables, it may be difficult to know what to try and what to leave well alone. Firstly, it makes little sense to grow food that nobody likes, so that it would just go to waste, On the other hand, it is just possible that the children will be tempted to try cabbage and other dislikes when they have contributed towards their production; they may even grow to like them.

Take a fairly relaxed view about selecting your crops. In the first season grow everything that captures your imagination, within reason. At the end of the season you will discover which grow best in your garden and which you prefer to grow, and you can therefore plan more knowledgeably for the following year. In making your assessment, however, do consider the effects of the weather. In a summer with little sun your tomatoes may have been a failure, few of them ripening by the end of September. But think carefully before allowing this to deter you from ever growing tomatoes again — the next summer may be a scorcher!

The site you choose for your vegetable plot should be open, and receive sun for at least part of the day. It should also ideally be fairly level and away from the base of large trees. We prefer not to see the plot situated too close to the house — decorative features provide a more pleasing view. If you feel that a vegetable plot may really spoil the appearance of the garden, then it can be screened by climbing plants on a timber support or a wall of open brickwork or decorative screen blocks, ensuring that the screen does not cast heavy shade.

The size of the plot will vary according to the needs of your family. Assuming that you are aiming to supplement and enrich the diet of your family of four, rather than establish total self sufficiency, then you can start with a plot measuring as little as 10 by 10ft. Much depends on the amount of time and effort you are prepared to devote to your crops. It can be very depressing and disheartening to find that you have embarked upon a course that proves too demanding. Better to keep your efforts to manageable proportions, particularly when you are beginning.

The best time to start planning your vegetable plot is in the autumn. Although you will not start sowing and growing until the following spring, this will enable you to get the soil into a good condition and provide a better start for your crops.

During late autumn or early winter the soil should be cleared of weeds and large stones and well dug, with manure, compost or peat added during the digging process. If the soil in your garden is clay and very heavy, sprinkle garden lime over the surface when you have finished digging, at a rate of 6 to 8oz per sq. yd, depending on just how sticky the surface feels.

When you dig, leave the soil in large, unbroken clods for the winter frosts to break down and form a crumbly consistency. The lime will help to break down heavy soil, and will be washed in by rain.

When you are ready to start sowing seeds in your plot in March or April, it is beneficial to sprinkle a general purpose fertiliser over the soil and work it in with a fork. Do this a week or two before sowing.

There are three basic ways in which your vegetables can be started. Some can be grown from seed sown directly outdoors; others must be sown in a protected environment, either in a greenhouse or indoors. However, where these less hardy crops are concerned, it is often much simpler for the beginner to buy young plants from a garden centre or shop. This is also true of crops such as cabbages, that have to be sown in a nursery bed and transplanted to their final positions. The plants will be available at a time of year when they can safely be planted directly outdoors, and you will have the added benefit of being able to seek advice on your crops from a knowledgeable plant salesman.

Sowing seeds outdoors

Seed sowing should start in early spring and continue according to the requirements of each particular

▲
Organic matter, such as compost, improves the condition of soil. To make compost, place vegetable waste from kitchen or garden in a compost bin; keep covered. Add a proprietary compost activator to speed the process of rotting down.

▼
To dig over your vegetable plot, take out a trench the depth of a spade and 9 in wide from one end (spit A) and transfer soil to the other end of the plot. The next strip of soil (spit B) should be dug over to fill the first trench. Proceed until the entire plot has been dug.

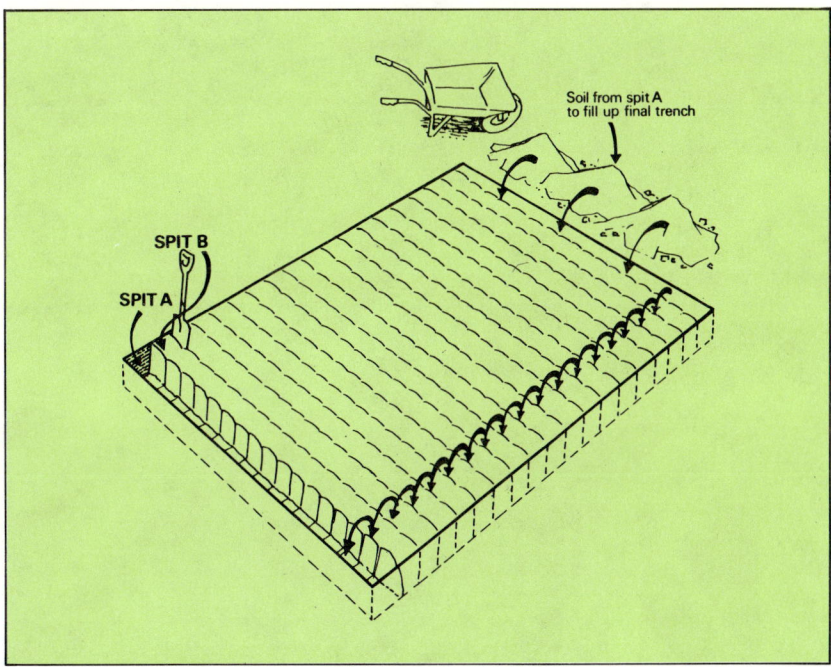

Soil from spit A to fill up final trench

SPIT B

SPIT A

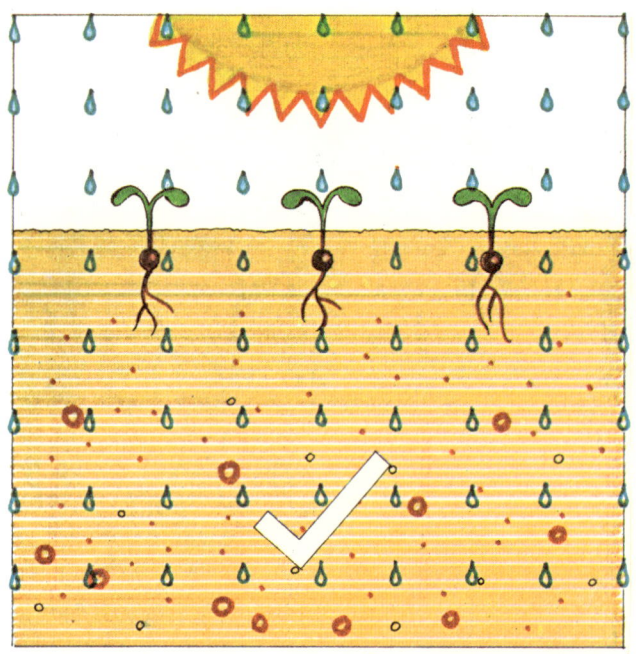 

▲
Germination of seeds depends on correct depth of sowing, condition of soil, warmth and moisture.

▼
Runner beans should be picked frequently and enjoyed whilst young and tender. Where space is restricted grow in a 'wigwam' or go for Dwarf French beans.

vegetable. Fast growing salad crops can be grown from successional sowings over three or four months, to ensure a continuous supply of fresh vegetables.

Sow your seed when there is no frost, and choose a fine, dry day. The soil should not be wet and muddy, but if it is very dry you should give it a watering the day before sowing.

Go over the soil surface with a fork, lightly breaking any lumps, then tread it to firm. If mud sticks to your boots, then the soil is almost certainly too wet to be raked ready for sowing, and you should wait for it to dry out a little more. However, if the surface starts to dry out and form a thin crust, then the time is right to rake the soil so that it is level and of a fine consistency. The seed bed should ideally run from north to south or from north-east to south-west in a windy garden, to protect the seedlings.

Mark rows in the plot by stretching a line of nylon or rot-proof string taut between a short stick at either end. Next make a drill to the depth required for the type of seed being sown, using a draw hoe or a piece of stick. The seeds should be sown thinly, and lightly covered; firm the ground with the head of the rake. In dry weather keep the seeds watered carefully, using a watering can with a fine rose to avoid washing the seeds out of their drill.

▶
Beetroot is not difficult to grow; crops picked in autumn can be stored throughout the winter months.

▶
Brussels sprouts should be grown in firm ground in order to produce small, tight buttons.

▼
Broccoli — a delicious vegetable that is almost always expensive to buy at the greengrocer.

1. Prepare the soil surface by using a fork to break up any lumps.

1.

2.

2. Then tread to firm; the soil should start to dry out and form a thin crust. Do not sow if soil is wet and sticky.

3. Rake the soil so that it is level and of a fine, crumbly consistency.

3.

4.

4. Mark rows with rotproof string and take out a seed drill to the depth required, using a draw hoe or a short stick.

5. Sow seeds thinly in the drill and lightly cover with soil.

6. Firm the soil covering with the head of a rake. Mark the end of the row with the name of the vegetable variety that has been sown.

5.

6.

When the seeds have germinated, and the seedlings are large enough to handle, thin them by pulling out the weakest, leaving the plants to grow at the spaces recommended on the seed packet. Do this in gradual stages to avoid total loss from any pest or disease that may strike.

Pelleted seed

Some vegetables have particularly fine seed that can be difficult to handle. Many seed suppliers now make pelleted seed available; these have a coating that makes them easier to handle, and therefore easier to space out accurately and to thin.

However, it is essential to keep the soil moist until the seedlings have developed; if pelleted seeds are allowed to dry out they may simply fail to germinate at all.

To protect seedlings from birds, we find that crumpled kitchen foil suspended from the end of a cane with string is quite effective, and the foil moves in the breeze, glistening and rustling over the crops. The traditional method is a length of black cotton along the row, or alternatively proprietary 'bird scarers' are available.

Sowing seeds indoors

Vegetables that need protection from the elements until early summer can be sown in a greenhouse, or in the house.

Fill trays or boxes with moistened proprietary seed compost; level and firm. Sow seeds thinly and lightly cover with compost. Cover with a piece of glass or sheet of polythene and grow in a warm place until the seeds have germinated. Turn the glass or polythene daily to avoid a build-up of condensation.

After germination, remove the cover and grow the seedlings on in a light position. When they have two or three open leaves, transplant the seedlings into individual peat pots filled with potting compost, such as John Innes. The pots should be kept moist, and not allowed to dry out.

As the weather becomes warmer, the young plants should be hardened off; take them outdoors in the day-time and bring them in at night for a week or two. They can be planted out in the garden when the nights are a little warmer and all danger of frost is past. The peat pots can be simply plunged into the soil in the garden, where they will rot away. This disturbs the plants' roots as little as possible.

Regional variations

The time for sowing and planting out vegetables may vary according to the part of the country in which you live. The soil in the south generally starts to warm up earlier in the year than in northern regions, and you should rely on your own commonsense as well as being guided by the advice given on seed packets.

A late, cold spring can have an effect on the whole country; do not be tempted to sow your seed while the weather remains very wet and the soil cold and sticky. Better to wait until the correct conditions prevail, and enjoy your crops a little later in the year.

Harvesting

As a general rule, it is preferable to pick or lift crops when they are first mature, in order to enjoy vegetables in the peak of condition, with a good texture and flavour. 'Little and often' is a valuable maxim; harvest a little from each sowing or plant at a time, and do so often.

Pests and diseases

A comprehensive survey of all the possible pests and diseases that could affect your crops would probably be so depressing that you would be deterred from growing vegetables at all! Nevertheless, it is wise to be aware of the problems that can occur, so that you can identify and speedily deal with them, or better still avoid them occurring where possible. Those affecting some of the most popular individual vegetables are dealt with in this chapter. Possible problems of other crops may be indicated on seed packets, and one or two garden chemical manufacturers produce information in the form of a chart or booklet.

Many people like to feel that one of the great benefits of 'growing your own' is the production of crops that are uncontaminated by chemicals or artificial substances. However, there is a middle ground between this philosophy and the methods of large scale commercial production. If your crops are threatened it makes sense to use a safe, proprietary chemical to save them from destruction.

New products that are safer and more effective are always appearing on the market, although these are often based on one basic, active ingredient. Always ask advice if you are in any doubt when buying sprays, puffers or liquids, to ensure that you use the right product for the purpose, particularly if your vegetables are nearly ready to eat.

How to grow some of the most popular vegetables in your garden

Beans — Dwarf French

Dwarf beans can be even more tasty than runner beans, and can be cooked and eaten whole. They need no support and stand up better to drought.

Varieties

We suggest 'Masterpiece', 'Loch Ness' and 'Tendergreen', which is stringless and excellent for freezing.

Culture

Sow seeds outdoors in early May, then make two more sowings at fortnightly intervals. Sow two seeds together 2in deep, 9in between pairs, and 18in between rows. After germination, remove the weaker seedling of each pair. Put down slug pellets to protect the seedlings from slug damage, and support the plants with twiggy sticks when they are becoming laden with beans, if necessary. Beans should be grown in a different part of the vegetable plot each year.

Harvest when the pods are about 4in long, from July to October. Pick 'little and often' and with care, so that the plant is not loosened from the soil.

Beans — runner

Varieties

'Streamline' — a good all rounder; 'Desirée' — a stringless variety; 'Enorma' — good flavour.

Culture

Sow seeds outdoors in late May. Sow two seeds together, 2in deep, 12in between each pair and 12in between rows. Make two more sowings at fortnightly intervals.

When each seed has germinated, pull out the weakest seedling of each pair. Support for the plants will be necessary to a height of 6ft in the form of string, net or canes; these can be placed to form a 'wigwam' where space is restricted. Keep well watered in dry weather, watering the base of the plants rather than the leafy growth. When the plant reaches the top of the cane, pinch out the top.

Blackfly can be a problem; spray with rotenone (derris) or other suitable insecticide. Harvest from August to October. Pick often; do not allow the beans to get too big. Beans are very good for freezing.

Beetroot

Quite an easy vegetable to grow. Storage of crops in autumn means that you can have freshly cooked and prepared beetroot with winter salads.

Varieties

'Detroit'; 'Boltardy'.

Culture

Sow the seeds in rows 9in apart, and thin to leave 4in between plants. Sow first in April, then every two weeks until the end of June.

Hoe between rows to keep weeds down and water in dry weather. Beetroot can be pulled from the time they are the size of a golf ball, from early July through the summer. In October dig up with a fork the beetroot still in the ground. Shake off the soil and take off the leaves, and store the beetroot in a box of dry peat in a cool, dry, frost-free place. Small, young roots can be frozen.

Brassicas

Vegetables classified as brassicas include cabbage, cauliflower, broccoli, Brussels sprouts and kale. They all require similar treatment when raised from seed, although young plants are generally readily available at the appropriate time. They should also be grown in a different part of the vegetable plot each year.

► Spring cabbages can be harvested early in the year for use as 'greens' or allowed to mature and picked in early summer.

► To help ensure clean, hearty cabbages, like this 'Drumhead' grow in a different part of the vegetable plot each year, alternating with peas or beans and root crops.

▼ Savoy cabbage is as good to look at as it is to eat!

Position cloches in early spring to enable early sowing of crops such as lettuce, and provide protection from cold wind and birds.

▶ Round rooted carrots have a sweet flavour if pulled when young and look attractive to serve at the table.

▶ 'Salad Bowl' — the lettuce that has no heart but a mass of crisp, curled leaves, so that you can cut as required.

If you decide to grow from seed, sow seeds in a 'nursery bed' in rows 6in apart, and thin the seedlings to approximately 1in apart in the row. The plants should be lifted, using a hand fork, when they show five or six young leaves; do this when the soil is damp, or in dry weather water the night before. Transplant the young plants to their final position in rows, 18in between plants either way. It is important to ensure that there is no cavity left under the roots, and that the soil is pressed firmly round the plants. Finally, water thoroughly.

Possible problems of brassicas
One of the most troublesome pests is the caterpillar of the cabbage white butterfly. Crush the eggs when they appear on the leaves in late summer, and if possible pick off the caterpillars. You can also spray with rotenone (derris), particularly the underside of leaves.
Cabbage root fly maggots eat the roots and stems of young plants. If they attack, the plants and the soil immediately around the roots must be dug up and burned. A precautionary measure is to dust the

soil around the plants with bromophos just after they have been transplanted.

Club root is perhaps the most serious of diseases, detectable by stunted growth and swellings on the roots. The best way of avoiding this is to grow brassica crops in fresh soil each year, returning to the original patch only after two years, and to add lime to the soil where brassicas are to be grown.

The simplest brassica vegetables to grow are:

Broccoli

Purple sprouting broccoli has two varieties; 'early' can be harvested from February to March and 'late' from April to May.

Green sprouting broccoli or calabrese is very useful, for the heads or spears are ready to harvest in autumn, and it is a delicious vegetable that is often expensive to buy at the greengrocer.

Culture

All seeds should be sown in April and transplanted in June.

Hoe between plants to keep the soil free from weeds whilst the plants are growing; some protection may be needed from birds when the plants are young.

Harvest at the times described above. Cut the spears when the heads are a mass of tight buds, and before they start to open. Broccoli can be frozen.

Brussels sprouts

Varieties

'Peer Gynt' — compact and therefore suitable for the smaller garden; 'Early Half Tall' for early crops and 'Irish Elegance' for freezing.

Culture

Sow in mid March to April and transplant in May, allowing 2ft each way between plants.

Ensure that the plants are firmed well in. Hoe between rows while there is space, and remove yellowing leaves in autumn.

Harvest from October to February; start picking from the bottom of the stem. Small, tight sprouts are suitable for freezing. When the sprouts have finished the leafy tops can be cut off and cooked as 'greens'.

Cabbages

There are many varieties of cabbage, for use virtually all the year round.

Varieties — spring

For spring use good varieties are: 'Wheelers' Imperial' — small, pointed hearts; 'Offenham — Flower of Spring'; 'Durham Elf' — medium to large heads.

Culture

Sow seed in late July to early August. Transplant September to October, allowing 6 to 9in between plants and 18in between rows.

Harvest in early spring for 'spring greens'. Remaining plants can be left at 18in spaces to form mature cabbages ready in April to June.

Varieties — summer

For summer use good varieties are: 'Greyhound' — an old favourite and 'Hispi'; both are pointed. 'Primo' and 'Golden Acre' are round varieties good for salad, and 'Ruby Ball' is a red cabbage suitable for pickling.

Sow in March and transplant in early June, 18in spaces each way between plants. Harvest from June to August, simply cutting as required.

Varieties — winter

For autumn and winter use good varieties are: 'Winnigstadt' — compact, pointed hearts; 'Savoy King' — beautiful to look at as well as good to eat! 'Christmas Drumhead'; 'January King'.

Sow in May and transplant during July at 18in spaces each way. Harvest from November to March, as required.

Carrots

Not a particularly easy crop to grow; carrots prefer rich, deep sandy soil. It is, however, worth persevering, as nothing you buy in the shops can quite compare with the taste of young, freshly picked carrots — particularly raw in salads.

Varieties

Best for flavour are the short or round-rooted varieties including 'Early Nantes' and 'Amsterdam Forcing'.

Good longer varieties are 'Chantenay Red Cored', 'Autumn King' and 'James Scarlet Intermediate'.

Culture

Seeds are very small, and pelleted seed is easier to handle. Sow in April outdoors; sow seeds ½in deep allowing 9in between rows. Thin to 4in apart.

Carrot fly can be a problem. As a precaution, dust the soil with bromophos before sowing. Flies are attracted by the smell of crushed leaves, so thin seedlings in the evening, after watering. Pelleted seed has a further advantage here, as seedlings require less thinning. Hoe between the rows regularly.

Harvest small carrots as they are required for use. In October lift all those remaining in the ground, remove the soil from their roots and cut off the tops to ½in long. Store these between layers of sand or peat in a box in a cool, dry, frost-free place, for use during winter.

Jerusalem artichokes

Not a commonly known vegetable, but one that is easy to grow and good to eat. Plants have tall, leafy growth rather like a sunflower and can be useful as a screen. The small, root vegetable is the part that is eaten, and looks rather like a small, knobbly potato. Try serving mashed with butter; tastier than potatoes and fewer calories!

Varieties

Plant tubers, available from garden shops or through a seed catalogue. Best variety is 'Fuseau', with long, smooth tubers.

Culture

Plant in March or April outdoors, 4in deep, 12in apart, in rows 2ft apart. Firm the soil around the tuber and water.

While the plants are small, hoe between them and keep the soil moist. When plants are taller you may need to tie lengths of string to posts at either end of the row for support and protection from wind.

In October the leaves turn yellow and the plants should be cut off to leave short stubs.

Harvest after the stems have been cut down by loosening with a spade and lifting the whole plant out of the ground. Leave plants in the ground until you need them, even in frost, but not later than the following February.

Lettuce

A really worthwhile vegetable to grow, being easy and available for many months of the year. Lettuce not only has high food value but it can be used as the basis of a simple side salad with almost any dish.

Varieties

Cabbage shape: 'Buttercrunch'; 'Avondefiance'; 'Great Lakes'.
Cos: 'Little Gem'; 'Giant Green Cos'; 'Lobjoit's Green'.
Curled, crisp leaves: 'Webb's Wonderful'.
Non-hearting variety: 'Salad Bowl' — produces no heart, but a mass of curled leaves that can be cut as required. Good for a crisp salad.
Winter varieties for early spring use: 'Winter Crop'; 'Winter Density' (cos).

Culture

Sow seed outdoors, just ½in deep in rows 12in apart. Sow half a row at a time, commencing in March and continuing at fortnightly intervals until July. Thin to a final distance of 9-12in apart. Pelleted seed is easier to handle. For over-wintering lettuces sow seed in late August-early September.

Care for the plants by putting down slug pellets and protecting young plants from birds. Greenfly should be sprayed with a suitable proprietary preparation. Grey mould can also be a problem; this is a fungus that attacks the plant at soil level, causing it to wilt. Sprays are also available to combat this.

Harvest lettuces from June to September, as soon as they have a firm heart. Pull up the entire plant and dispose of the roots and lower leaves. Over-wintering lettuces can be harvested in early spring.

Marrows and courgettes

Marrows are useful vegetables to grow, since one makes a meal for the whole family. Increasingly popular nowadays — and rightly so — are courgettes, which are baby marrows cut when they are just about 4in long, and cooked whole or sliced and fried in butter.

Varieties

For marrows: 'Green Bush'.
For courgettes: 'Zucchini'.

Culture

Marrows need a sunny but sheltered position, as they are not hardy plants. They also need rich soil, and it is preferable to dig out a hole approximately 12in by 12in, and fill this with a mixture of compost and soil before sowing or planting.

Sow seeds outdoors in late May. Sow three seeds in a group 1in deep to each prepared bed, allowing 2ft between beds. When the seeds have germinated, select the stronger of the three seedlings and leave this to grow on; pull out the weaker two.

Put down slug pellets when the plants are young, and when the fruits begin to grow feed with a general purpose liquid fertiliser every two weeks. It is essential to keep plants well watered in dry weather. Harvest in August to October; cut fruits as soon as they are usable to encourage further cropping. Some large, mature marrows can be cut in October and stored in a dry, airy place.

Onions

Spring onions for salad

Spring onions are especially suitable for salad, and these are quite easy and quick to grow.

Varieties

'White Lisbon'.

Culture

Sow seed in March, and then at monthly intervals to give a continuous supply of spring onions for summer salads. Pelleted seed can be easier and safer to use, as it reduces the risk of onion fly. Sow seeds ½in deep in rows 9in apart. Hoe between rows and water in dry weather.

Harvest the onions from June to September by simply pulling up those with small bulbs ready to eat.

Onions for cooking

These can be difficult to grow from seed; a simpler solution is to buy onion sets, which are immature bulbs grown especially for planting out.

Varieties

'Stuttgarter Giant'; 'Rijnsburger'.

Culture

Plant sets in April 6in apart in a shallow drill, allowing 12in between rows. Partially cover with soil so that the necks are still showing; firm the soil around them.

Hoe carefully and water in dry weather. When the onions grow large and swollen, stop watering and let them ripen in the sun. In about the middle of August the leaves of the plants will start to bend; two weeks later they will be ready for lifting. Do this with a fork on a dry day and spread the onions out in the sun to dry. They can be stored in a dry, airy place in trays or net bags.

Peas

Peas can be a somewhat difficult crop to grow, and can take up quite a lot of space. There are early, maincrop and early maincrop varieties, cropping at varying times throughout the summer. The early varieties are probably best for the smaller vegetable plot, as they grow to only about 18in high and are sweet tasting.

Cos varieties of lettuce have a firm heart and crisp, crunchy leaves.

Onions are best grown from sets — immature bulbs that should be planted out in April.

Pepper plants thrive in a warm, sunny, sheltered position. Where space is limited they can be grown in pots or even decorative containers on the patio.

Radishes are one of the easiest vegetables to grow, and mature quickly from seed.

Varieties
(Early) 'Kelvedon Wonder'; 'Little Marvel'.

Culture
Sow seeds outdoors in March. Take out flat drills approximately 6in wide and 2-3in deep. Sow seeds in three rows in the base of the drill, 3in apart in all directions; allow 18in between drills. Cover with soil and firm.

As soon as the seedlings are 2in high, hoe between the rows to aerate the soil and keep down weeds; protect seedlings from birds. The plants may need support in the form of twiggy 'pea sticks'. Water thoroughly in dry weather.

Harvest in June and July, picking from the bottom of the plant. Pick the pods regularly.

Peppers
The sweet pepper or capsicum is worth growing if you have a suitably warm, sunny sheltered position in the garden, as it is a very tender plant. Peppers may not succeed outdoors in northern or colder parts of the country.

Varieties
'Canape'; 'New Ace'.

Culture
Sow seeds indoors in April; plant out in the garden when the plants are about 4in high. Alternatively, buy plants for planting out in early June, 18in apart each way, or in pots.

Keep plants well watered in dry weather. When the flowers appear, spray plants with water. When the fruits begin to form, feed the plants with general liquid fertiliser once a week.

► Choose early varieties of peas; they are sweet tasting and grow to only about 18 in high.

► Where space is restricted, the ideal way of growing tomato plants is in the now familiar growing bag.

► Spring onions can be sown in succession from March onwards, for a continuous supply throughout the summer.

Harvest from August to September; pick peppers when they reach a good size.

Potatoes

Like peas, potatoes can be grown for early or mid-season harvesting. Most worthwhile for the small vegetable plot are the early varieties, for these are ready when new potatoes are still expensive in the shops. What is more, their flavour is superb, and they can simply be washed before cooking and boiled and eaten in their tender skins, with butter.

Varieties

Early varieties include 'Foremost'; 'Duke of York'; 'Arran Pilot' and 'Epicure' — particularly good for flavour.

Culture

Plant seed potato tubers. Small tubers about the size of an egg are best; order these early and when you receive them (probably in February) stand them in a seed tray in a light, frost-free place with the end where most 'eyes' can be seen pointing upwards. The eyes will start to shoot; take care not to break off the shoots.

In late March-early April dig out a trench approximately 5in deep, and one spade's width. Space tubers 12in apart, and allow 24in between rows. Cover with soil.

When growth is about 6in high, 'earth up' by drawing soil up to the row, first along one side and then the other to form a ridge. Hand weed and hoe until the foliage of each row meets.

Havest from June to July when the flowers have withered; the potatoes can be lifted with a fork.

Radish

One of the easiest vegetables to grow, cropping quickly and plentifully through the summer to add piquance to salads.

Varieties

'Cherry Belle' — round.
'French Breakfast' — cylindrical.

Culture

Radish will grow in most types of soil. Sow seeds in drills ½in deep, with 6in between rows. Sow thinly, allowing about 1in between seeds. Sow in succession from March to May at fortnightly intervals.

Seeds germinate in five to eight days and radishes will be ready to harvest in four to six weeks from the time of sowing.

Tomatoes

Not a difficult crop, but tomatoes are tender and need a sunny, sheltered position. If your vegetable plot is too exposed, grow in pots or growing bags on the patio.

Varieties

Standard varieties grow with four layers or 'trusses' of fruit. Popular ones include 'Ailsa Craig'; 'Moneymaker'; 'Eurocross'; 'Outdoor Girl'; 'Marmande' (large, fleshy fruit).

Bush varieties are even easier, as they grow to only approximately 2ft high and need no support. Varieties: 'The Amateur'; 'Sleaford Abundance'.

Culture

Sow seeds indoors in late March or early April to plant out in early June, or buy plants. These should be about 8in tall and look sturdy, with dark green leaves.

When planting in the garden, allow 18in between plants.

Standard varieties need a strong 5ft cane placed close to the plant for support; tie the plant to it at 12in intervals as it grows. As the plant grows, side shoots will appear in the join of the stem and leaf stalks; these should be pinched out. When four trusses have formed, pinch out the top of the plant two leaves above the fourth truss to prevent it from growing any taller.

Bush varieties need no support, and side shoots do not need to be pinched out. However, you should lay polythene on the ground around the plants, as some fruit grows at ground level.

All tomatoes should be watered consistently. Do not allow plants to dry out, as this results in the fruits splitting later. When the fruits start to form, feed every seven to ten days with a liquid tomato fertiliser.

Harvest fruits by picking when they are ripe. At the end of the season, fruits just beginning to ripen can be picked and stored in a cool, dark place wrapped in tissue paper. Those that are still green are usually relegated to the pot for making green tomato chutney.

Growing vegetables in a restricted space

If you have a very small garden, or one that is almost entirely paved over, it is still possible to grow a few vegetables. One of the biggest recent developments in this area has been the now ubiquitous growing bag. There can be few simpler ways of growing tomatoes, peppers or courgettes than buying a bag and two or three plants in early summer, simply opening the bag, transplanting the young plants and giving water and liquid fertiliser as required. Plastic grids are now available to assist still further; these fit around the bag and provide support for taller plants such as tomatoes and aubergines.

Vegetables can also be grown in large flower pots or even decorative containers; this is true of French and runner beans, as well as those mentioned above. Herbs are a particularly attractive crop for a large container; they are easy to grow either from seed or young plants, and most will last for some years, although some are annuals.

Mint can be invasive, and should be grown alone, but basil, chives, fennel, marjoram, rosemary, sage, tarragon and thyme will all grow together in a warm, sunny position (parsley prefers a damper, shady spot).

One or two pots of herbs placed on the patio near to the kitchen will prove convenient when you want to pick herbs for adding to casseroles, sauces, salads, soups or stuffing. They will also exude a pleasant aroma on warm, summer evenings.

Growing fruit

Growing fruit in your garden is quite a different proposition from producing a few vegetables. The production of fruit is not a question of experimenting with quick crops on a 'trial and error' basis, but represents a permanent, long-term investment with trees and bushes being nurtured to maturity. On the other hand, it is not necessary to sow and plant every year, as with vegetables, and you can extend the sense of satisfaction felt at eating home-grown, freshly picked fruit.

There is no doubt that fruit has a

► **Creating a framework of branches**

After planting a new tree, shorten the strong side growth by one third to one half, in winter, removing lower branches that are weak or damaged.

After three or four years the well-shaped tree has a good framework of branches.

Winter pruning

► 'Cox's Orange Pippin' — a favourite eating apple that ripens November-December.

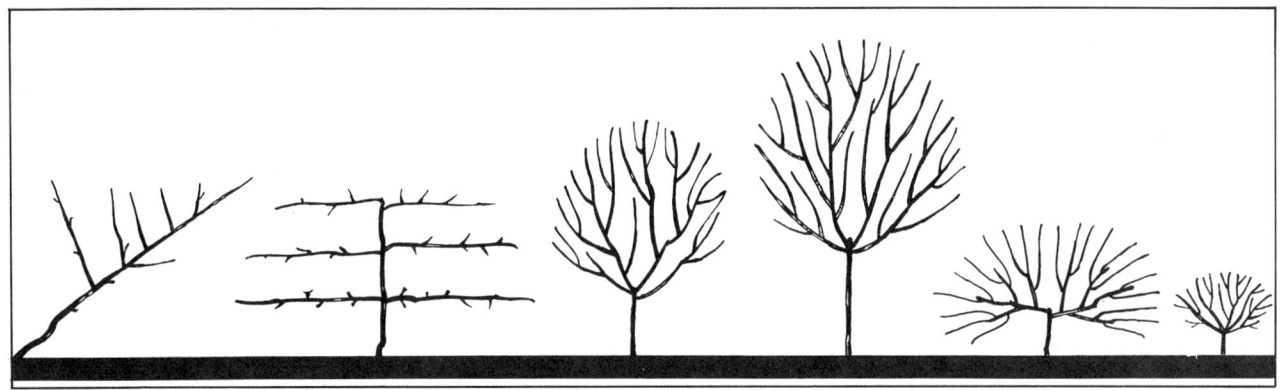

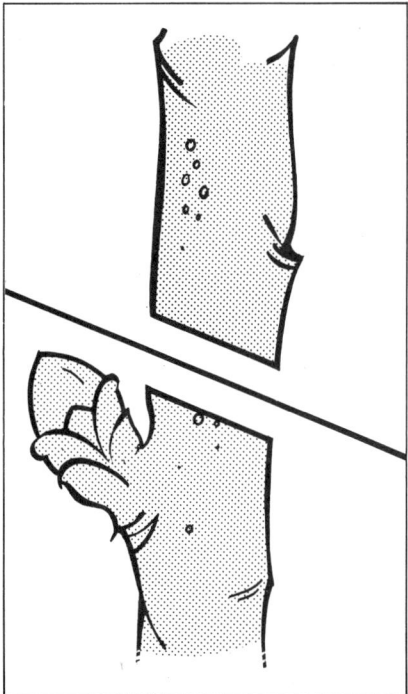

The shape of the framework of a fruit tree will usually have been established before it is sold. Those generally available are (left to right).
Cordon
Espalier
(Neither of the first two are recommended for the novice gardener.)
Half-standard
Standard
Fan trained
Bush

► A container grown apple tree can be planted at any time of year except when the ground is frosty or waterlogged.

► Detail of how to prune, making a clean, sloping cut just above an outward pointing bud.

better flavour when it is eaten fresh from the bush or tree. You can appreciate it in the peak of condition, and have easy access to varieties of soft fruit in particular that are in the shops for a short season at constantly high prices. Surplus produce can, moreover, be stored by freezing or bottling, or in the form of jams and jellies.

Fruit can be divided into two basic categories; top fruits grow on trees and include apples, plums, pears and peaches, and soft fruit grows on canes or bushes and include gooseberries, raspberries, blackberries, black and redcurrants and strawberries. The types you decide to grow will depend largely on personal preference and the amount of time and space that you have available.

Looking first at top fruits, the trees on which they grow should be considered as a year-round asset to your garden in a decorative sense, with their blossom in spring, leaves in summer and even the attractive shape formed by the bare twigs in winter. You can, therefore, plan their position in the garden much as you would any other tree; it is not necessary to allocate a plot for top fruit. Ensure that the tree is planted at a suitable distance from the house.

Fruit trees should also be in a sunny position where possible, to

98

protect the blossom from late frosts. Indeed, some varieties can only be grown in warmer parts of the country, others are better suited to colder areas, and you should check when buying or ordering. Whatever the variety of the fruit you decide to grow, you will have to select the size and shape of tree you are going to plant.

A standard tree, which usually has a 6ft stem, should be considered in the same way as any other deciduous tree that will grow to a fair size, and should be allowed a similar amount of space; trees should be planted at a minimum distance of 25ft from each other. If you want a tree that will produce fruit quickly, this is not a good choice, since it will take several years to mature. If, on the other hand, you want to have all the benefits of a sizeable garden tree, with the added advantage of fruit in abundance in a few years' time, then a standard will be ideal.

The half-standard has a stem of 3½ to 4ft clear of branches; this makes it slighly more manageable for pruning and picking, but a distance of 20ft between trees is still required.

A bush tree has a very short stem of about 2 to 3ft, with an open-centred head of branches. This is a very much more practical consideration for the small garden,

particularly if you do not want to wait too long for your first crop of fruit. There is also a greater possibility of planting more than one tree since a distance of only 12 to 15ft between bush trees is necessary. Moreover, a ladder will not be needed for picking fruit and pruning the tree.

If there is space for only one or two trees in your garden, you may find it difficult to narrow down the choice of fruit that you want to grow, or wish to avoid a glut of one particular variety. The answer here can be a 'family tree', a tree that is formed by the grafting of three different varieties of apple or pear on to one root. The result is a half-standard or bush tree that produces smaller quantities of each fruit over quite a long period, for the varieties are planned to complement each other in timing and use.

Top fruit trees are also sold in the form of cordons — a single, straight, narrow stem — and espalier — a vertical stem with tiered horizontal branches. However, we would not recommend either for the newcomer to fruit growing. They require a considerable amount of pruning and care in both summer and winter, and if allowed to grow too quickly can produce a lot of leaf and little fruit.

▼

To remove a large branch, start at a point 8-12 in out from the trunk. Make an upward cut in the bottom of the branch to prevent the bark from splitting, then saw through. The remaining stump can be neatly sawn in the same way. Trim the wound with a sharp knife to tidy, and paint with a proprietary wound sealant.

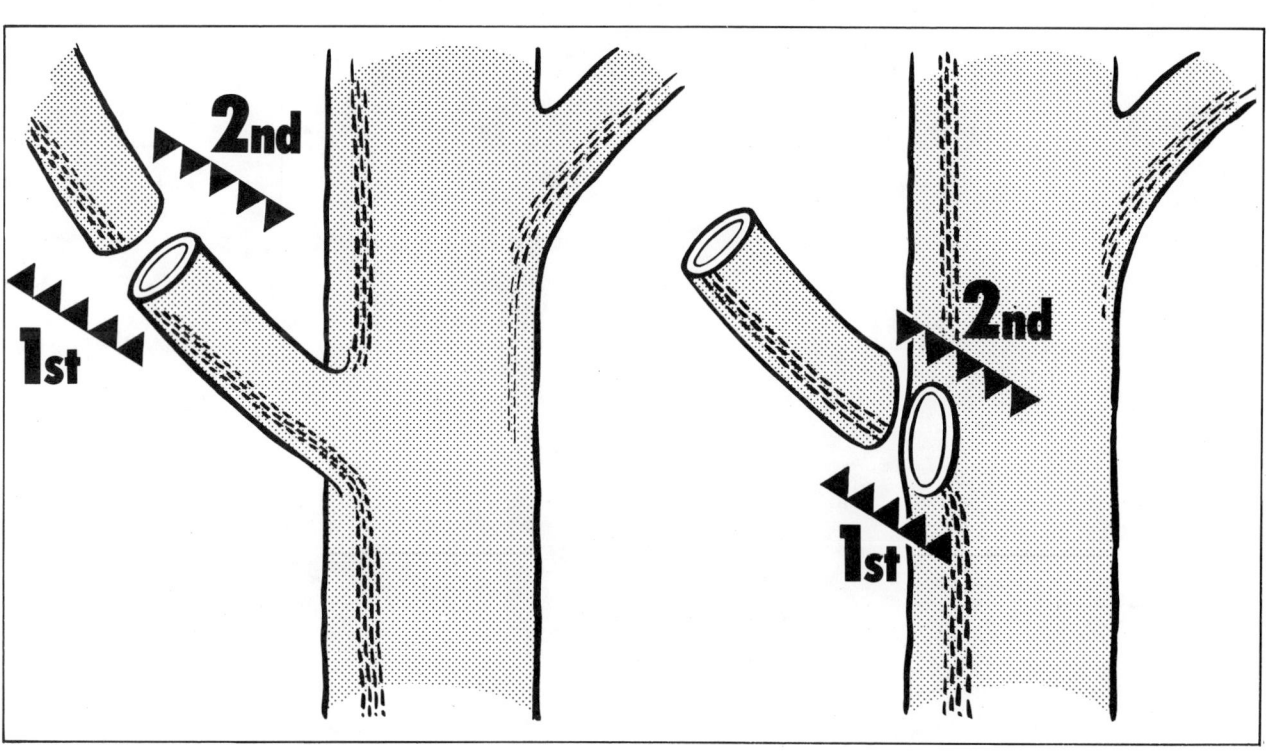

Buying and planting a fruit tree

The process of planting is much the same as for any tree, in that the soil should be well dug and prepared, and a good large hole is needed to accommodate the roots. Fruit trees do require soil with good drainage, but will tolerate soil that is not rich, cooking apples and plums being the least fussy. A stake will be needed for support.

Take care to plant the tree at the depth at which it has been growing in the nursery. The join where the fruit variety has been grafted on to the stock shows as a lump near the base of the stem, and this should

►

'Discovery' — an early ripening dessert apple with a good, slightly sharp flavour.

▼

The familiar 'Conference' pear has long, russet coloured fruits.

be 2 to 3in above soil level. Keep the tree well watered in at least the first season after planting, and thereafter during any periods of very dry weather.

Trees are available from nurseries and garden centres in container grown or bare root form. The former can be planted at any time of year except in periods of very dry weather or frost, and open ground trees can be planted in autumn, winter or early spring, but again not when the ground is frosty or waterlogged.

The tree you buy may have been pruned before it is offered for sale (check when buying); if not, you will need to prune it to encourage new, strong growth. If you plant a container grown tree in late spring or summer, you should wait until the tree has lost its leaves in autumn before pruning.

Look for the tree's main 'leader' shoots and cut off approximately the top one third of new growth, using a sharp pair of secateurs; make a sloping cut. Then find the short, woody stems or 'spurs' that actually bear the fruit, and cut them to leave two or three fruit buds; these are the plumper, rounded buds.

A further object of this first pruning is to create a framework of branches that will form a well-shaped tree, continuing the work already done by the nurseryman. If a new tree is pruned too lightly, it will bear too much fruit in the first season and put on little growth, and this could result in a mis-shapen or stunted form.

► An established plum tree should be pruned sparingly; tackle re-shaping of a neglected tree over a period of time.

► Blackberries are easy to grow and can be trained to clothe a wall or fence attractively.

Pruning established apple and pear trees

Pruning is sometimes regarded with a degree of trepidation by the newcomer, who feels that he is going to cause some irreparable damage to the tree, and therefore tends to leave well alone. In fact, there is no mystery to the methods of pruning, and the process is best approached with a degree of logic, and an understanding of the basic aims behind it.

Pruning an apple or pear tree can be carried out at any time between November and March, when the tree is in a dormant state, but the best time is in November, as soon as the leaves have fallen.

To prune a bush tree, first cut off any shoots that look diseased and unhealthy. Then single out one branch at a time and, starting at the bottom, prune the side shoots. These are the new shoots that have grown out along the branches during the summer. Side shoots that are short and sturdy can be left, but any that are longer than 4 or 5in should be cut back so that only two or three buds are left.

The 'leader' shoot is at the top of the branch. This is the new, young growth and only about one third of it should be cut; do not be tempted to prune it hard back.

Cut the leader shoot to a bud that is pointing in the direction in which you want the branch to grow, so that the tree keeps a good shape and all the branches have sufficient space to develop.

Spurs are short, woody and branched, and they should be spaced at approximately 5in intervals along the branches. Any spurs that look too long and weak should be pruned to leave just two or three of the plump flower buds.

In order to ripen, the fruit on the tree must receive air and sunlight. As the tree gets older, you may see that the branches are too crowded for sufficient light and air to penetrate, and side branches that are crossing and cramped should be removed.

Standard and half-standard apple and pear trees require a similar treatment to that of bush trees for the first few years, but once they become more established, it will only be necessary to thin and shape the tree. The main aims should be to remove branches that are diseased or dying, and to prevent the centre of the tree from becoming too overcrowded.

Should any large branches need cutting out, the cuts should be made with a sharp saw, and the wounds painted with a proprietary sealant. This helps the wound to heal quickly and prevents further disease.

Pruning plum trees

A newly planted plum tree should be pruned in much the same way as newly planted pears and apples. However, established plum trees must be pruned only sparingly. The spurs can be allowed to grow quite freely, and the leader shoot only needs to be cut lightly when the growth is very vigorous.

It is important that diseased, dying and awkwardly placed branches on a plum tree should be spotted and cut out when they are young, and still quite small. It is a more risky operation to cut out large, thick branches, but if this is absolutely necessary it should be done in midsummer and not in winter, so that the risk of infection by disease is reduced. Should you inherit an established garden with an old, neglected plum tree, do not attempt to carry out mass amputation of branches all at once, but tackle the re-shaping gradually, removing just one or two large branches each year.

Pollination

One important point to bear in mind when you are selecting a variety of apple, pear or plum is that very few can be fertilised by their own pollen. Most must be cross-pollinated by a different variety in order to set fruit really successfully. If you have a sufficiently large garden for more than one tree, plant varieties that will cross-pollinate with each other (they do not need to be planted particularly close together). You can check on suitable varieties when buying.

If there is space for only one tree in your garden, then look around for fruit trees in neighbouring

> Pruning is done to remove unhealthy shoots, to let sunlight and air into the tree and to encourage the development of more fruit.

gardens, and if you can ascertain the variety, plant one that is complementary. Alternatively, it will be necessary to plant one of the few varieties that are self-pollinating to a sufficient degree. Self-fertile dessert apples are 'Ellison's Orange' and 'Laxton's Superb', and cooking apple, 'Grenadier'. For a plum choose 'Victoria', and for pears plant either 'Conference' or 'William's Bon Chrétien'.

Pests and diseases

There are various pests and diseases that can attack top fruit, some of them common to all types and others restricted to only one variety. Among the most common pests are aphis (green or blackfly); caterpillars; codling moth maggots found in fruit and woolly aphis, white woolly masses on branches and shoots.

Diseases include canker — hollows in the bark surrounded by swollen wood; mildew — a powdery white covering on shoots and leaves; and scab — dark, sooty blotches on leaves and fruit.

There are proprietary chemicals to deal with all of these, and you should seek the advice of a knowledgeable salesman for answers to particular problems. Prevention is better than cure, and this can be effected by spraying with a tar oil wash in winter, when the buds are dormant. The other basic treatment is the application of a combined systemic insecticide and fungicide in summer.

Soft fruit

Soft fruit grows on canes and bushes. Whilst it is necessary to set aside an area of the garden for some, such as blackcurrants and gooseberries, a row of raspberry canes can prove useful as a screen of medium height, and blackberries and loganberries can be even more useful, for they will clothe a fence or wall, and are not unattractive garden plants.

Popular types of fruit include:

Blackberries
Varieties

'Himalayan Giant'; 'Oregon Thornless' — a variety with no thorns that produces heavy crops of sweet tasting fruit.

Culture

Blackberries and the hybrid varieties will grow almost anywhere against a support, particularly in the form of a fence or wall, or even a pergola. Plant at any time from October to March

---

Recommended varieties to look for:

Dessert apples

'George Cave' — good flavour fruit with a red flush. Ripens July-August.

'Worcester Pearmain' — crimson fruit; pick only when ripe. Ripens July-August.

'Ellison's Orange' — juicy fruit but does not keep. Ripens September-October.

'Cox's Orange Pippin' — the old favourite. Ripens November-December.

'Laxton's Superb' — sweet, juicy fruit. Ripens January onwards.

Dessert and cooking apples

'James Grieve' — crisp, yellow fruits with red stripe. Ripens September-October.

'Blenheim Orange' — excellent flavour. Ripens November-December.

Cooking apples

'Bramley's Seedling' — another old favourite, with a high vitamin content. Ripens November-December.

'Arthur Turner' — beautiful flowers as well as good apples. Ripens September-October.

Pears

'Beurre Hardy' — tender fruit with excellent flavour. Ripens October-November.

'Conference' — familiar long fruits with russet skin. Ripens October-November.

'Doyenne du Comice' — large pale yellow fruits, deliciously juicy. Superb flavour. Ripens October-November.

'William's Bon Chrétien' — long yellow fruits; a reliable cropper. Ripens August-September.

Plums

'Czar' — cooking plum that is easy to grow. Ripens in August.

'Coe's Golden Drop' — delicious, large, juicy fruits; dessert. Ripens late September.

'Victoria' — popular and familiar variety for dessert or cooking. Ripens September.

with a space of 10 to 12ft between plants, and 6 to 9ft between the thornless varieties.

Prune the canes to 9in above ground level if this has not already been done; new shoots will appear and these should be tied in to the support to form a fan shape. As the plant matures, allow new canes to grow upright in the centre of the plant. Fruiting canes that have already been trained to fan out should be cut back after the fruit has been picked, and the new young growth can then be fanned out from the centre to take its place.

Blackberry hybrids

Although blackberries grow wild in this country — even in some gardens — the cultivated varieties produce more fruit. There are a number of close relatives of the blackberry that are interesting to grow and rather more unusual.

The loganberry is supposed to be a cross between the blackberry and the raspberry; it produces nice large fruit with a popular, distinctive taste. The thornless Boysenberry is becoming increasingly common in this country, having been introduced from America. The fruit is large and purplish black in colour, with a superb flavour, and is produced in abundance.

The Japanese Wineberry is smaller than a raspberry, and makes a more decorative garden plant. Berries are yellow, turning red when ripe, with a deliciously sweet taste.

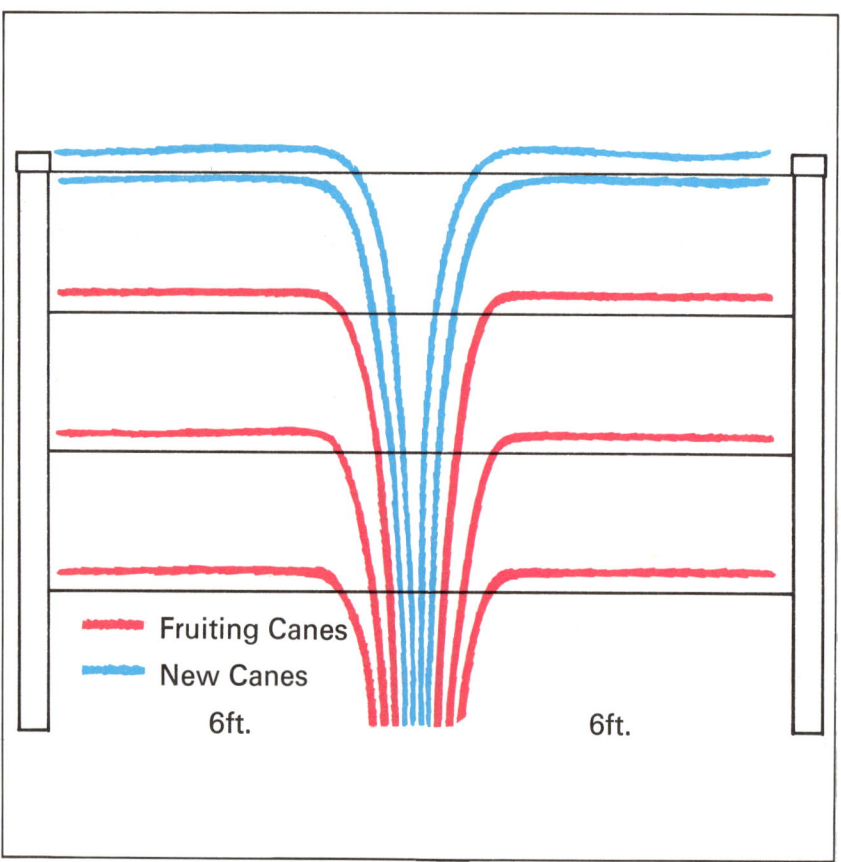

Fruiting Canes
New Canes
6ft.   6ft.

► Fruited canes of blackberry are cut back after picking to allow new canes to be fanned out from the centre of the plant.

► The loganberry produces large, luscious red fruits.

104

► Diagrams showing how to prune an established blackcurrant bush.

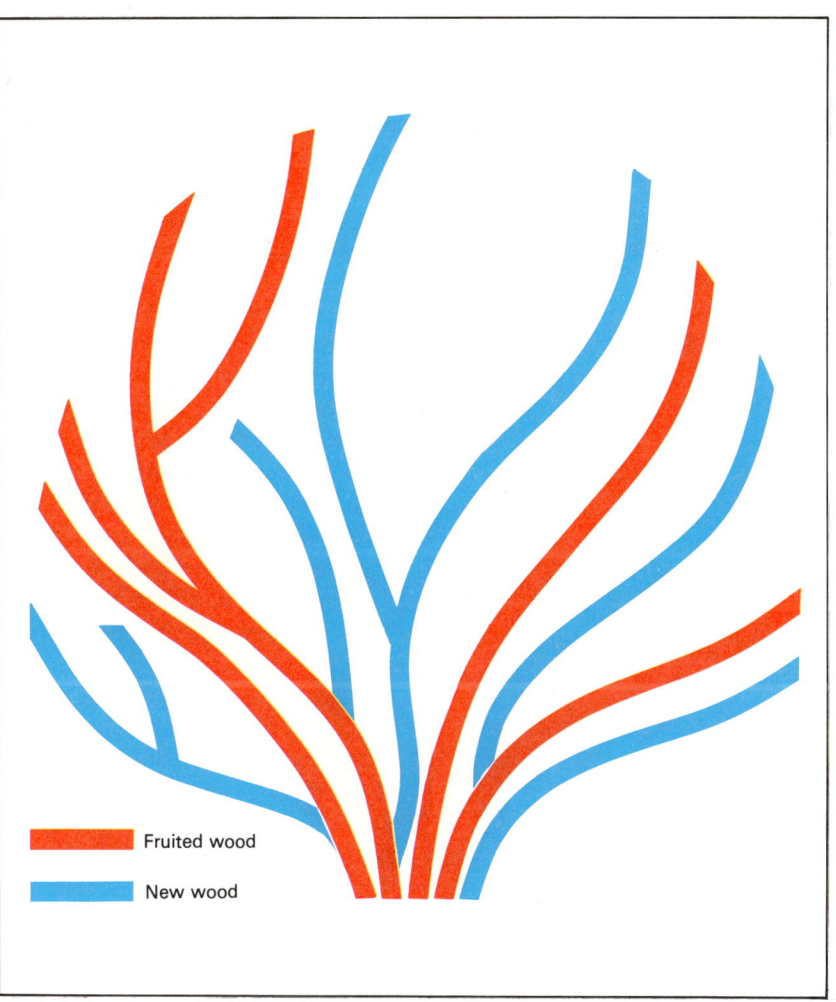

Fruited wood

New wood

Blackcurrants
A valuable source of vitamin C as well as a tasty fruit.

Varieties
'Baldwin'; 'Boskoop Giant'; 'Wellington XXX'.

Culture
Position should ideally be sunny, but partial shade is tolerated. Protection from wind is important, and a rich, well manured or composted soil is required.

Plant the bushes any time from October to March, although autumn is ideal. Allow a space of 5 to 6ft each way between plants (about 5 plants is sufficient for a family of four). After planting cut all the shoots down to 1 to 2in above soil level, to encourage new growth from below the ground. These will bear fruit in the second summer after planting.

When the bushes are established, prune by removing the oldest branches, the aim being to encourage as much new growth to emerge as possible, for this will produce the best crop.

Keep blackcurrants well watered and apply a proprietary general fertiliser in February.

Gooseberries
Gooseberries are not difficult to grow. Their requirements are similar to those of redcurrants, and they can be grown close by.

Varieties
'Careless' — cooking; 'Leveller' — dessert; 'Whinham's Industry' — red fruit for dessert or cooking.

Culture

Gooseberries should ideally be planted in full sunlight, but as with other soft fruits a degree of shade is tolerated. Shelter from wind is required.

Prepare the soil by adding peat, manure or compost and also sulphate of potash at the rate of 1oz per sq. yd. Plant bushes allowing a space of 5 to 6ft between plants each way. Cordon gooseberries are a good idea where space is restricted, as these can be planted at only 1ft spaces.

Plants are prey to damage from birds, particularly bullfinches, who like to eat the buds in winter. They should therefore be covered with a fruit net during winter months if possible.

Prune bushes to form a framework of strong, upright growing branches, but keep the lower part of the stem clear of growth. If any suckers should appear from below ground level, pull these right out. When the plants are established, prune in March, cutting the main shoots back by one half of their length.

Raspberries

It is well worthwhile growing raspberries, for they are not difficult and produce an abundant crop once the plants are established. The soft, melting fruit is delicious eaten freshly picked and surplus quantities can be bottled, frozen, used as flavouring or for jam making.

Varieties

Summer fruiting — 'Malling Jewel'; 'Malling Promise'; 'Glen Clova'.
Autumn fruiting — 'September'; 'Zeva' — fruits right through to November.

Culture

Raspberries prefer an open, sunny position in the garden, but they will tolerate partial shade. They should be planted well away from the roots of trees, as their root system is rather shallow and sparse and may become starved of food and moisture. The soil should be well drained, as waterlogging can kill the plants. Finally, raspberries should be provided with shelter from wind, which can damage plants by causing them to pull out at the roots.

Raspberries are easily obtainable in the form of canes from garden centres or specialist nurseries, and can be planted at any time from late October to March, although autumn is the best time. The ground should be well dug, incorporating compost, peat or manure and it is important to ensure that the ground is free from weeds.

Before planting, bang a stake into the ground at either end of the row where the canes are to grow, and stretch lengths of wire between the stakes to provide support (the stakes should be 5ft tall above the ground). Plant canes firmly, allowing 18in between plants and 5 to 6ft between rows.

After planting, prune the canes if this has not already been done, by cutting them down to 6 to 12in above soil level. Keep plants moist. At the end of the first summer after planting, cut the old canes down to the ground and leave the new canes that have formed to grow on; these will fruit the following summer.

When the plants are established, prune when all the fruit has been picked, for summer fruiting varieties. Cut down all the old canes that have fruited and leave the six strongest new canes to form the crop for the following year; these should be tied to the wires as they grow.

Pruning of autumn fruiting raspberries is a different process. The young canes that form during the summer should be left all through the winter, and all should then be cut down to ground level at the end of February.

Redcurrants
Varieties

'Laxton's No1'; 'Red Lake'.

Culture

Prepare the ground and plant as for blackcurrants. Pruning is a different process. When the bush

Before planting raspberries dig deeply, adding compost. Raspberries need plenty of moisture as the fruits begin to swell.

has been planted, cut off each branch to 3 or 4in, just above an outward pointing bud; this will encourage new, fruit bearing shoots. When the plant is established, prune in winter by cutting back the side shoots, leaving two or three buds, and cutting about 6in off the main, leading shoots.

Redcurrants are particular favourites of birds, and it will be necessary to protect the plants by covering them with a fruit net in winter and in summer when the fruit is forming, although this should be removed when the bushes are in flower.

Rhubarb

The part of the rhubarb plant that we eat is, of course, the stem rather than the fruit, and plants are generally treated more like a permanent vegetable crop. Buy crowns, in the form of large roots with several buds, and plant them 2½ft apart each way in autumn or early spring. Plants appreciate a rich soil in an open position away from trees, and should be watered well in the first season after planting, and thereafter in dry weather.

The stems will not be ready for picking until the second spring after planting. When you pick, give the stems a gentle twist. Feed plants occasionally with a general liquid fertiliser in summer and remove flower stems as they appear.

Strawberries

Strawberries are, of course, an essential feature of the English summer, and it is well worth growing a few plants. They are encouraging to grow as fruit can be produced in the first year after planting, and you can gain a delicious reward for relatively little work. There are three types of plant; the summer fruiting, the 'perpetual' fruiting and the Alpine strawberry.

Varieties

Summer fruiting: 'Cambridge Favourite'; 'Grandee'; 'Tamella'.

Culture

Plant in a sunny position, having dug compost into the soil. The best time to plant open ground plants is in late summer or early autumn, for fruit the following summer. It is possible to plant in spring, but if you do so, pick off any flowers that appear in May and wait until the summer of the following year for a really good crop. Pot grown plants can be planted in spring to flower the same summer, because their roots will not have been disturbed.

Allow spaces of 12 to 18in between plants, and 2ft between rows. Plant firmly so that the crown of the plant is just on ground level. Water the plants every day until they become established, and if they lift out of the ground with winter frosts, firm them back in. When the flowers have died and the fruits start to form, give the soil a really good watering every week or so.

Weed between the plants and lay polythene on the soil around them when the fruit is swelling, to keep the strawberries clean.

'Runners' will appear in the form of small, off-shoot plants from the parent plant. These can either be pulled up and discarded or allow them to root and replant them as new stock in August. Never take runners from plants that are diseased.

Immediately after all the fruit has been picked, remove the polythene from around the plants, and, using a sharp knife, cut off all the leaves and burn them in order to minimise the risk of perpetuating disease. New leaves will soon start to appear. On the question of disease, any plants that have stunted growth, discoloured or crinkled leaves should be dug up and destroyed. Proprietary sprays and dusts are available to deal with most pests and diseases to which strawberries are susceptible.

Perpetual strawberries

The perpetual fruiting plants produce fruits from June to October. The main plant itself fruits first, and then the runners fruit in the autumn, until the first frosts, although the main crop is

Protecting soft fruit from bird damage by growing under a netting cage is worth consideration.

▲
Raspberries are not difficult to grow, and produce an abundant crop once the plants are established.

►
'Grandee', a heavy cropping variety of strawberry that produces enormous fruits.

▼
Cloches protect strawberry flowers from early frosts. Polythene laid on the soil keeps the fruit clean.

picked in August and September. Plant in autumn or spring and remove flowers until July.

Varieties
'Rabunda'; 'Gento'.

Alpine strawberries
The variety most commonly offered for sale is 'Baron Solemacher' which is, strictly speaking, a relative of the alpine strawberry. It is extremely useful as a small garden plant, for it is tolerant of shade and can be planted under larger subjects. Plants produce tiny fruits right through the summer.

Strawberries in pots
Strawberries are very well suited to growing in pots and tubs on the patio, or even in a window box. We like to see them in the traditional terracotta strawberry pot, with several cup shaped openings, but a more modern alternative in the form of a tall plastic 'tower' planter is becoming popular. Containers should be of a minimum 10in depth and a similar width.

► To prune summer fruiting raspberries cut out all the old canes that have fruited, after harvesting.

► Leave four to six strong new canes and tie these to the wire supports as they grow.

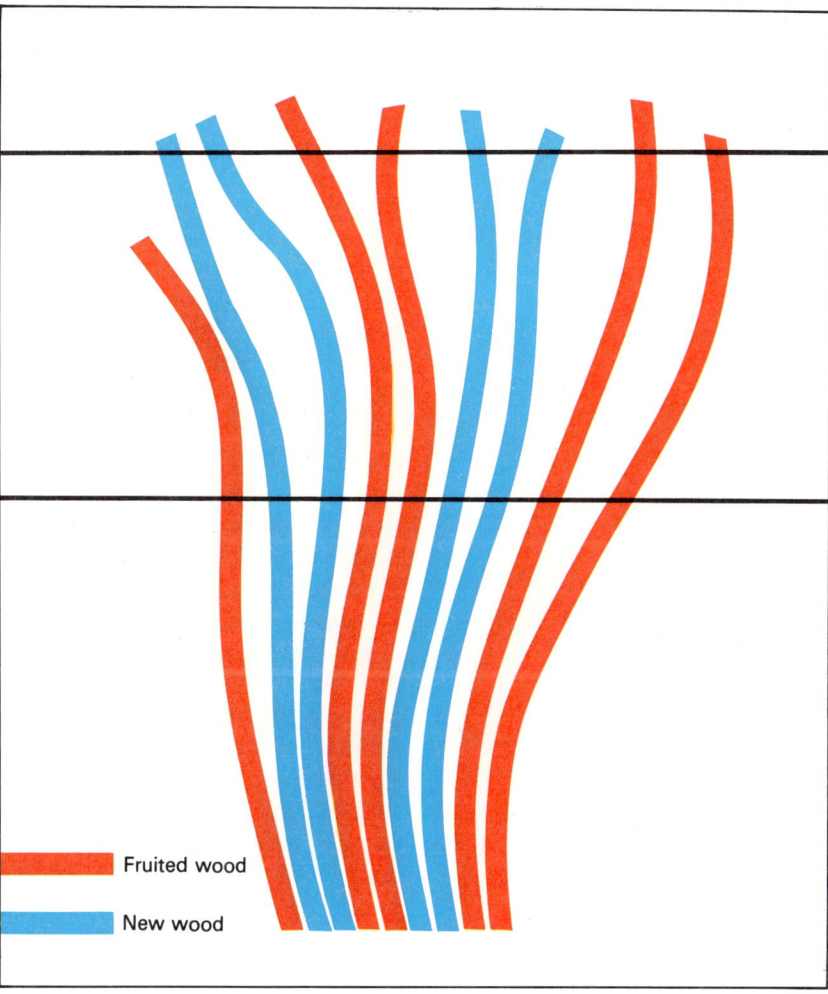

Fruited wood

New wood

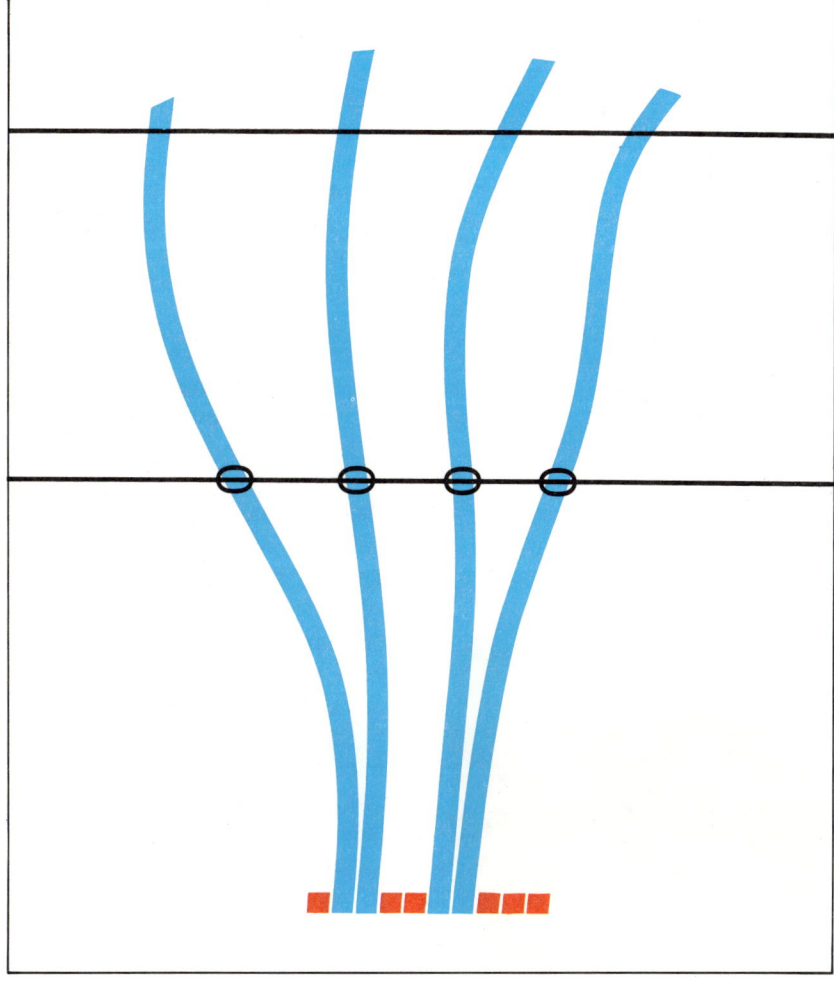

Leisure in the garden

A garden that is well planned and laid out should not only look beautiful, but should also be convenient and enjoyable for all the family to use. If your garden is really to become an 'outdoor room', then everything should be on hand to induce you to simply step outside to spend your leisure time, rather than driving long distances away from home.

Of course, you may not be able to afford to equip your patio in the manner of a smart dining room, but any investment you do make should prove well worthwhile. Relaxation in your own garden is a unique experience, for there you can not only enjoy looking at the fruits of your labours. Your garden can become a personal, private sanctuary — a peaceful haven for a few hours, away from the bustle of everyday working life.

Relaxation can take many forms. For some, nothing helps them to unwind more than the hard work of gardening. It becomes a positive pleasure, rather than a chore, to cut the grass or dig over the vegetable plot, and it's certainly good exercise! For others, their idea of heaven is sitting back in a chair listening to the birds singing and the hum of life quietly going by. If this appeals, the first obvious requirement is that the chair in which you sit should be a comfortable one.

But comfort is not the sole consideration. If the garden is seen as outdoor living space, then the furniture and accessories should, as we have said before, complement the design and mood of the layout, and the style of your house, just as you would expect them to do indoors. Indoors you have complete control over setting the scene, but in the garden there is an added dimension, for the appearance of the furniture should blend with natural surroundings, and not create too harsh a contrast to plants and decorative features.

Garden furniture

Chairs made from collapsible tubular metal with striped canvas or nylon may be about the cheapest form of outdoor furniture, but they are not really very satisfying to look at.

When considering your choice of outdoor furniture, decide whether you are likely to use the garden for sunbathing or snoozing, to sit and read, to take jobs and activities like sewing or sketching outdoors, or for outdoor meals.

If you plan to spend a lot of time sunbathing, perhaps a sun lounger would be the most appropriate choice of furniture; this can be taken outdoors as required.

However, for most families an outdoor set of table and chairs that are always readily available for use would be a more practical proposition. This means the selection of a material that can be left permanently outdoors; perhaps only the cushions need to be taken in to protect from bad weather.

Treated timber is, of course, weatherproof, and it blends with almost any outdoor setting, being a natural material. A simple, fairly rugged rustic style would best suit an informal layout or a country garden. Most good garden centres and large stores have a selection of slatted, stained or varnished timber tables and chairs or stools. Wood is often a very expensive material, but prices vary and it is possible to find something reasonably priced that is nevertheless quite durable.

Several manufacturers market a 'picnic table' unit with integral benches, and this can be good value, although less flexible than a separate table and chairs. For the more sophisticated town garden, painted timber is rather stylish. This is usually sold painted white, but you could have fun painting the furniture in a colour to complement your garden scheme. Plastic, too, is weatherproof, and

we feel that it is best used to make furniture in simple, modern, moulded forms. There has been a boom in plastic coated metal furniture in Victorian-style patterns during the last few years, but this seems to be less popular now.

The intricate Victorian patterns can blend nicely into a garden setting since they are so often based on leaf and flower designs. The original pieces were probably made in cast iron, at a time when the use of solid metal was popular and widespread. However, light-weight aluminium has become a more acceptable modern material for its dual benefits of lower cost and easier manouvreability.

Co-ordinating accessories

If you are going to use the garden for outdoor meals, why not co-ordinate all your accessories. This need not involve a great deal of extra expense — merely the exercising of imagination and care when buying. For instance, if you have upholstered chairs with

➤ Owning a garden need not be all hard work. Take the opportunity to sit back and relax in a peaceful haven — and enjoy the fruits of your labours!

A garden seat that blends perfectly with its surroundings. In a sheltered position, it is convenient for lounging or taking small jobs outdoors.

The summer-time rewards of work done earlier in the year. Choosing flowers to decorate the house is always a pleasant and relaxing occupation.

► Lightweight plastic furniture has a bright, modern look and can be left outdoors ready for use.

► With sheltered, brick-built barbecue and comfortable furniture in natural wood, the scene is set for stylish outdoor living.

your table and plan on buying a large parasol to shade the table and protect food from direct sunlight, ensure that the fabric of the parasol either matches that of the upholstery, or picks out a single colour in the pattern. In this way, the entire setting will look as though it is designed to go together, rather than the individual items having been added piecemeal, almost as an afterthought.

When it comes to the crockery that you use, you may not want to take the best china outdoors, just to make the table look nice. However, you can find low priced plastic table or picnic ware in bright, primary shades that will add a splash of colour to your table setting. The finishing touches can be added by paper napkins, also in a matching colour.

Of course, it is doubtful that you would be so enthusiastic about living graciously that you would take the trouble to ensure that the table looks exactly right every time you take a tray of tea outside. But if you have all the necessary accessories on hand, you will find that you spend more time outdoors because you can take meals out with relatively little fuss and upheaval. You may also feel more confident of inviting visiting friends and relatives to eat on the patio, in the knowledge that you are able to 'do things properly'.

If you are a keen do-it-yourselfer, you will possibly resent paying the price charged for a set of timber furniture that you could make at less cost and without too much difficulty. Your knowledge should enable you to find ideas than can be adapted and modified from ready-made garden furniture and from specialist magazines. It can also be fun to convert items that others would regard as 'junk'; you can still find the solid, ornate metal bases of old-fashioned sewing machines and these make a perfect small table for the garden with a timber or even marble top from an old dresser.

Consider also installing 'built in' furniture to your patio, as an integral part of its design. This will means that a seat outdoors — either timber or stone — is always handy, thus encouraging frequent use of the garden.

Barbecues

The interest in barbecuing has obviously increased in this country, during the last few years, because an increasing number are sold every year. Nevertheless, the enjoyment of outdoor meals cooked on a barbecue can hardly be said to have become part of our way of life.

There are probably several reasons for this apparent resistance to an enjoyable activity. Firstly, we tend to be cautious of anything different, often seeing the barbecue as essentially an American activity or better suited to youth clubs and girl guides. Secondly, the weather puts us off. We tell ourselves that hot, dry weather can be relied upon so infrequently that it simply is not worth the effort.

Finally, we cannot contemplate enjoying a barcecue in the garden if we feel exposed to the view of the neighbourhood, or if our own garden is an overgrown mess or barren waste that does more to put us off our food than to further its enjoyment.

Neither of the first two objections is really valid. A barbecue can be great fun for a small group of family and friends, and we generally enjoy at least a few hot, sunny days or warm evenings in the course of the summer. As for the lack of a pleasant, sheltered garden in which to appreciate the food, this entire book is devoted to helping you overcome that particular problem!

The cost of buying a barbecue and the necessary accessories varies from a few pounds for a simple metal fire-bowl and grill for the table top to hundreds of pounds for a trolley-mounted grill that is powered by calor gas cylinders. Barbecue models that are portable or fold-away are also available.

The basic principle is the same — the charcoal burns at a high temperature to cook the food above it on the grill. Grill heights are often adjustable, and accessories such as a rotary spit for chickens can be added. A whole range of tools and gadgets are also available,

but initially you can almost certainly manage with ordinary kitchen utensils.

When positioning your barbecue, try to find a sheltered spot where the wind is blowing away from your family or guests. A further safety factor is that a lighted barbecue should never be left unattended. In any event, it is wise to have a bucket of water on hand, in case of disaster.

Charcoal can be readily obtained in pre-packs. Also obtainable are barbecue firelighters, and these should always be used in preference to paraffin and methylated spirits, which can be dangerous and spoil the taste of the food.

As regards the food for your barbecue, you will find it easier to cook only one item of each course by this method — usually the meat or fish. Have salads, sauces, bread and other accompaniments ready in advance for guests to help themselves because you will need to devote your full attention to the barbecue cooking.

Barbecued meat need not be the best steak. Try home-made beef-burgers, using good quality minced beef, lamb cutlets, hot dogs or chicken drumsticks. You should trim any excess fat from meat, since this can drip into the fire and cause a flare-up.

A built-in barbecue on the patio will always be ready for use, and add a touch of luxury. Use bricks or manufactured walling blocks (these are now available in a barbecue kit form) to build up a simple box, with adequate shelf space for charcoal and a grid built in to the top course of brickwork. This should finish at waist height, to make it convenient for cooking, and can form part of a unit with a 'table top' surface immediately beside it, and even a cupboard underneath for storage of charcoal and tools.

Garden lighting

Your barbecue will not be very pleasant — or safe — if everyone is groping in the dark, unable to see what they are doing. The answer to this problem is some form of garden lighting.

Lighting does not only make your garden more usable after dark, it also extends the time available to you to enjoy looking at the beautiful setting you have created. And if there are parts that you would rather not see — well, leave them in darkness. The nice thing about lighting is that you are in control, and can highlight only the most desirable features of your garden layout.

It is possible to achieve a range of effects, depending on the position of your lights. For example, if a specimen plant is lit from behind, its silhouette will be highlighted, but if it is bathed in a gentle glow from the front, the details of flowers and foliage will be picked out. These can take on an intriguingly different appearance in artificial light, due both to the colouring and the depth of light and shadow. It is also important to achieve a balance of intensity between indoor and outdoor lighting, since bright indoor lights will prevent you from seeing anything but reflections in the window.

Lighting can be a useful safety factor, showing up a step or an object that people are likely to trip over, particularly in the front garden, and beside entrances.

There are several ways of illuminating the garden, some permanent, others of a more temporary nature for a special occasion. High powered lights can be installed as permanent fixtures, but it is essential to ensure that cables are of the correct material and properly earthed and laid so that they are safe and weatherproof. Most manufacturers recommend that they should be installed by an experienced electrician.

A much simpler form of outdoor lighting is a group of low voltage lamps. These are readily available from garden centres and stores, and work on a safe, straight-forward principle. A lead is connected to a convenient electrical socket indoors, and runs to a transformer, which converts the power to a very low voltage. Weather-proof cable leads from the transformer into the garden, and lamps can be fixed at any point along the cable. This can be tacked on to a

115

Mushroom lights are a permanent feature of this garden, illuminating the terrace and attractive areas of rock and planting.

For small children the garden is a whole new world to explore; full of fascinating shapes, colours and movement.

A large, open area of lawn gives scope for children to play outdoor games, such as badminton, that will keep them amused for hours.

wall or concealed just beneath the surface of the soil. Lamps have brackets for wall fittings or spikes for fixing in the garden.

A selection of four or five interchangeable filters enables a choice of four colours, but it is generally most effective to stick to a colour scheme. Use either a combination of cool blue and green to highlight leaf colours (a lamp can even be concealed in a plant's foliage) or the warmer glow of red and orange, which can pick out flower colours or the tones of brickwork.

A rock feature is always worth looking at after dark. Rocks, like plants, can take on quite a different character; a new, almost mysterious dimension is added to their appearance. One fascinating way of introducing lighting to the rock garden is in the form of 'light rocks'. These are large, artificial pebbles made from moulded, textured fibreglass. A low wattage bulb is concealed inside the mould, and a lead runs to a socket indoors. The 'rocks' cast a very gentle glow, and are available in varying sizes; a group provides a real talking point!

A pool with waterfall or fountain looks particularly attractive with lights playing on the dancing water, and this can be achieved by positioning lamps on spikes in the ground beside the pool. However, it is possible to add an extra dimension by the use of sealed, waterproof lamps that are designed to be submerged beneath the pool water. These lamps run from a transformer on the same principle as the regular outdoor lamps, and are supplied in pairs. They cast a soft, diffused glow, again in a choice of colours, that can add a magical quality to your pool. However, we feel that it is best to avoid using a combination of many colours, since these will tend to create an effect that is more appropriate to a seaside resort.

Temporary lighting

If you are having a barbecue outdoors, or want a summer party to spill over into the garden, then it is possible to add temporary lighting for the occasion. Coloured, slow burning patio candles are sold in protective glass

containers and these can either stand on a table, or hang from a tree, wall or even the washing line in a specially made bamboo holder, giving something of an oriental look to the garden.

Many outdoor candles have the added bonus of being insect repellant. This can be very useful for midges, gnats and other nocturnal insects can spoil everyone's enjoyment of the great outdoors.

If you want a pretty, reasonable form of lighting for a party, try floating a couple of burning candles in a bowl of water, with just a single perfumed flower for decoration. Another very cheap form of temporary lighting is the use of flares. These should be placed in a heavy bottle on a firm base, and allowed to burn slowly. Their flicker will add atmosphere and a touch of excitement to the proceedings.

Play equipment

If you have a young family, the chances are that one of the most important requirements of your garden is that it should be a place where the children can play constructively, safely and for long periods of time without getting bored. There should be the facilities for them that will avoid the eternal cry of 'I'm bored — I don't know what to do'.

Of course, children should be encouraged to use their imagination when playing, and often they gain greater enjoyment from a game of their own invention than from pounds' worth of sophisticated equipment. It is the old story of the box being played with more than the toy that it contained. But it can be useful in the long term to provide areas and facilities that are the domain of the children, on the understanding that they steer clear of the vegetable plot or the roses that are father's pride and joy.

Under fives particularly enjoy the basic, all-time favourites — sand and water. Allowing them to indulge their strong urge to feel, touch and play with these elements helps them to develop an understanding of the relation of their own body to the world around them.

You will want to keep a watchful eye on children of this age, and so it is practical to plan a sand pit near to the house — perhaps as a feature to one side of the patio. It can take the form of a free-standing plastic tray that could be emptied when not in use or a built-in construction that can later be converted to an ornamental pool. This should have allowance for drainage of rainwater. It helps to have a flat surface beside the sand pit where children can sit or line up a row of sand pies.

It is essential to use the fine, washed silver sand for playing, not the yellow builder's variety, for this would tread and stick and cause yellow staining on children, house and garden. It is also a good idea to make a timber cover for the sand pit to prevent it from becoming a haven for cats at night. A cover also comes in useful from the aspects of safety and appearance if you want to use the garden for a more sophisticated, adult barbecue after dark.

Paddling and swimming pools

When it comes to the introduction of water for play, the way in which you do this will probably depend on two factors — cost and space. If you have strictly limited supplies of both, then all is not lost. Toddlers can be quite happy playing in their now disused baby bath. There is space for paddling, and floating boats and other toys.

The next stage is a small paddling pool that can be placed on the patio and filled with water when the weather is suitable, and emptied at the end of the day. The inflatable variety are not really ideal; they are exhausting to inflate and easily susceptible to damage. A better design is a plastic pool with a collapsible, folding surround that can quickly and easily be unfolded ready for filling straight away.

A full scale below-ground swimming pool is great fun for all the family. Owning your own is, however, a real luxury and comes at luxury prices. A properly constructed concrete or vinyl liner pool will cost several thousand pounds including accessories, and regular running costs will also be incurred.

Closer to the reach of most people is an above ground pool that is large enough for the children — and even their parents — to splash about in on a hot day and also, very importantly, sufficiently large for young children to learn to swim. In fact, they should never be allowed to play unattended in a pool of this size unless they are able to swim properly.

There are various types of pool available, made from either plastic in a rigid moulded form, or PVC sheeting on a metal frame. They can be installed and fitted for the summer, and stored away during winter months.

Position your pool in the garden where it will receive maximum sunlight, so that the water — and you — will keep as warm as possible. Avoid the proximity of tree branches.

Play areas

For older children who do not need to be kept under a watchful eye whilst playing, it is a good idea to set aside an area of the garden where they can do as they please within reason. This may not be possible in a very small garden, but where space permits it can help to lead to a peaceful co-existence between members of the family.

It is probably best for parents to resign themselves to the fact that a play area is unlikely to remain clean and tidy for long. Plan, therefore, for the ornamental part of the garden to be close to the house, and the play area in a less obtrusive position.

Sophisticated play equipment can be extremely expensive to buy and install, and children tend to grow out of it, as well as tiring of familiar games for periods of time. It can, therefore, be preferable, as we have said, to consider installing basic, multi-purpose items that become the starting point for any number of games and situations. In our experience children have a natural inclination towards the impromptu, exciting idea. Left to their own devices, they — exasperatingly at times — have no room for the concept that because a toy has cost a great deal, it must be played with at every opportunity.

Summer fun. Swings and a paddling pool turn the garden into an exciting playground that can make day trips to the coast almost unnecessary!

► Owning your own below-ground swimming pool is a real luxury, but it can provide hours of enjoyment for the whole family.

► Sowing sunflower seeds is an excellent gardening activity for children, since it produces such spectacular results for their efforts.

An element of danger also appeals, although we would not suggest you would allow them to put themselves in any real danger of injury. It is simply that an old car tyre suspended by a rope from a sturdy tree branch can be more exciting than a shining new piece of equipment. Another idea is to position upright logs firmly, so that youngsters can have fun jumping from one to another. Narrower timber stakes can be placed vertically, with their ends concreted into the ground, to form a palisade that will become anything from a wild west fort to a battleship. A rope ladder can also be fixed to a sturdy tree branch.

Very conscientious parents who are confident of their children's good sense — and head for heights

Moreover grass is unlikely to survive at all on the ground immediately beneath play equipment in frequent use.

Paving is more serviceable, but will also inflict more cuts and bruises on the inevitable occasions of falls and tumbles. Pea shingle can be quite a good compromise, although this may tend to be scuffed into other parts of the garden.

It is encouraging if you can persuade children to see the garden as something more than a playground, by developing their interest in plants and flowers. They will be more likely to respect your own efforts to create a pleasant environment or to grow fresh fruit and vegetables, if they

▶ Older children may develop a keen interest in gardening activities and can make a useful contribution to general maintenance and the care of plants.

— may even build a tree platform or house. Choose a strong position for it; the ideal place is in the centre of the tree, where the main branches meet.

Children love to have their own garden 'hideaway'. The addition of a shed, or hut to the play area will provide shelter and a storage space, both for bikes and larger toys and for the numerous grubby little items that they cannot bear to, throw away and you cannot bear to have in the house!

Choosing a ground surface for the play area can be difficult. Grass tends to become a mud flat in wet weather, although it is a pleasant, soft surface on which to play,

have experience of growing for themselves.

Set aside a plot that can be used as the children's own garden. Here they can sow seeds, plant bulbs and indulge in their own brand of decoration. Children are impatient, and will want to see a good return for their efforts, so it is a good idea for them to sow seeds that will grow quickly and easily like radish, or will produce a spectacular plant like sunflowers or nasturtiums. The garden can be decorated with shells and coloured pebbles from the beach, twigs made into flags and numerous other applications of everyday outdoor objects.

There is a wealth of life in the garden that is fascinating to observe and enjoy. Birdsong is one of the most delightful sounds of nature, and garden birds can be very interesting creatures.

It is easy for gardeners to complain about the damage that birds can cause to crops being cultivated with loving care, but on balance birds do more good than harm. Nearly all the smaller wild birds live on insects and their larvae during summer months, and thus help to control harmful pests.

The balance between successful cultivation of your garden and the enjoyment of the birds that visit it will be better maintained if you provide a suitable supply of food and water. Hungry birds are more likely to cause mischief! However, it is not very sensible to go out of your way to attract birds to your garden if you have a cat.

A bird table can take the simple form of a wooden tray mounted on a pole some 4ft high, 18in of which should be fixed in the ground. This should be placed in an open position nine or ten feet away from hedges and bushes, to prevent cats from lurking near it.

Garden birds like to eat household scraps, particularly fat meat, including bacon rind, and shredded suet; ensure that the meat has been cooked. Brown bread is popular, and also cheese, but do not put out more than can be eaten in one day to avoid attracting rats and mice. Nuts, in the form of cob-nuts, peanuts or coconuts will be eaten avidly — not only by tits — but avoid hanging out a coconut during the nesting season, as the young birds are unable to digest it.

Berries and flower seeds also attract birds. If you grow michaelmas daisies and sun-flowers, do not cut the dead flowers in autumn, but allow them to remain as a source of food. Thrushes and blackbirds are particularly fond of berries, and these supply food during the lean winter months. Suitable berry bearing trees and shrubs include holly, rowan, hawthorn, contoneaster, berberis and pyracantha.

Birds also appreciate a source or clean water in which to bathe all through the year. Ideally, it should be in a large, saucer shaped container so that they can walk in and out of the water. You may even find that they are attracted to a small garden pond.

Small birds may be induced to make their nest in your garden if you put out a nesting box at the appropriate time of year — about the middle of March. Make the box of wood, about 10in high with a sloping lid decreasing to 8in at the front.

A round hole in the front of the box of 1½in diameter will attract nuthatches, tree sparrows, blue tits or great tits to make their nest there, and a larger square opening will be preferred by robins.

Fix the box to a tree or a wall, facing away from the midday sun. If birds nest in it, they will probably produce several clutches of eggs during the season. They should be disturbed as little as possible, and certainly neither the adult bird sitting on the eggs, nor the eggs themselves nor the fledglings should be touched.

Although less spectacular than birds, butterflies and bees can also be attracted to your garden if the right plants are grown. A common name for buddleia is the butterfly flower, because butterflies — in particular the Red Admiral — are attracted to its large, heavily perfumed blooms. But they are also attracted to ivy and to the blossom of pear, plum and apple trees. Thistles and nettles are haunts of the Red Admiral and Comma butterflies, but few people would consider the cultivation of these in their garden a desirable feature.

Bees are attracted to flowers that produce pollen profusely. If there are beehives near your garden, you will be doing their owner a service by growing such flowers, since a bee is said to make three journeys to bring one drop of nectar to the hive.

Flowers beloved by bees are often perfumed, and also often blue in colour. They include forget-me-not, foxglove, campanula, scabious, honeysuckle and hollyhocks of the summer flowers, and wallflowers and heathers are favourites at other times of year.

If you wish to encourage birds and insects in the garden, there is a wide range of plants which are attractive to them.

▲
A songthrush with nestlings. Birds are an important part of garden life; their song is a delight and on balance they do more good than harm within a garden.

◀
The large, heavily perfumed blooms of buddleia are a favourite with butterflies.

Birds will be encouraged to visit the garden if food is supplied on a raised table. Positioned near to the house, it can be seen all year round.

Berries of shrubs such as cotoneaster provide a valuable winter source of food for birds.

Index